T0128243

THE MIRACLES OF
JESUS
Positioning
Yourself for a Miracle

PETER NEGRON

WESTBOW
PRESS®
A DIVISION OF THOMAS NELSON
& ZONDERVAN

Scripture taken from the NEW AMERICAN STANDARD BIBLE®, Copyright © 1960, 1962, 1963, 1968, 1971, 1972, 1973, 1975, 1977, 1995 by The Lockman Foundation. Used by permission.

WestBow Press books may be ordered through booksellers or by contacting:

WestBow Press
A Division of Thomas Nelson & Zondervan
1663 Liberty Drive
Bloomington, IN 47403
www.westbowpress.com
1 (866) 928-1240

ISBN: 978-1-9736-3196-5 (sc)
ISBN: 978-1-9736-3197-2 (e)

Library of Congress Control Number: 2018907372

Print information available on the last page.

WestBow Press rev. date: 06/29/2018

I want to thank my wife, Marilyn, and my family for their patience, support, love and encouragement during the writing of this book. I am not a writer or a theologian; I am a Christian and the Pastor of Pure in Heart Church in Franklin Park, Illinois. As a Christian and a pastor, I have had many experiences with the grace and power of Jesus Christ that I feel God has led me to write about in this book. It was written with the desire to encourage people with needs to have faith in God and His word. As I have said in the book, He is the same yesterday, today, and forever. The days of miracles are not over.

I would like to thank those who helped me with this project: Gary L. Finkbeiner from Kingsway Community Church and Reach the Nations, for his encouragement and advice; J. L. Rivera Logos Christian College in Jacksonville, Florida; Michael Peters for permission to use some of his work on miracles; and Melissa Finkbeiner from Kingsway Community Church in Grand Rapids Michigan, for their help with editing this work. I would also like to thank those who reviewed this work and gave constant encouragement, Ian Rossol of Leicester Christian Fellowship, Leicester, England, UK, and Victor L. Davis. And I want to thank the Pure in Heart church family for their prayers, encouragement, and support.

Dear Peter,

I have just finished reading your manuscript, *The Miracles of Jesus: Positioning Yourself for a Miracle*. I want to congratulate you on writing such a faith-building and inspiring book. I was challenged and motivated all over again as I read the stories—both from the Scriptures and also your own testimonies.

I love the way you consistently express your theme—that we have to position ourselves to receive. This book is such an encouragement not to grow weary in doing this.

Reading the book was like I was listening to you tell me the stories. Your heart and faith come through the pages. You do not make it complicated (for you are not a complicated man!), but it is truly real, and you make it accessible for others.

My personal conviction is that you should get this book published.

With love and appreciation to you and Marilyn,

Love,
Ian

Dr. Ian Rossol
Senior pastor
Leicester Christian Fellowship
Leicester, England, UK

Hi Peter,

You have done a great service to the body of believers by putting together the biblical accounts of miracles and healings that give clear testimony to the desire and willingness of Jesus to divinely lift the human/natural sufferings from those who position themselves in faith and cry out to Him, either for them or for others.

I was directly impressed with the statement that infers that "although *we don't know* why God doesn't always grant us miracles when we ask, *we do know* He has revealed to us that it is His intent to work miracles."

This is such a relevant and rich insight that I am convinced I will carry it with me throughout the rest of my life.

Vic Davis
Founding pastor
Spirit of God East
Gary, Indiana

I have known Pastor Peter Negron for over thirty years as a colleague and friend. His humble approach to scripture inspires others to faith. In this book, he tells the gospel story. In the illustrations and experiences, he relates how these spiritual truths have come alive in his life and ministry.

Anyone reading this book will be encouraged to believe that God wants to manifest Himself in lives today. His presence and power are available to transform lives and heal brokenness.

I look forward to seeing this in its final printed version.

Dr. J. L. Rivera
President
LOGOS Christian College
and Graduate Schools
Jacksonville, Florida

Contents

Miracles

When it comes to the issue of miracles, we need to understand that every time a miracle or healing occurs, it is a sign. It is a sign that points people back to God and to His ability to heal those He has created.

Miracles are also a callback to a relationship with Jesus Christ. We live in a fallen world, and people are broken and in need of salvation, healing, and miracles. So when Jesus performs a miracle, He is demonstrating His rule over all crated order.

When Jesus came, He not only fed people's souls with the truths of heaven and Him as the bread of life, but He also filled their stomachs with fish and bread and wine.

He opened not only the eyes of people's heart to see the truth but also their physical eyes, restoring their sight so they could see the world around them.

He strengthened the faith of the weak while strengthening the legs of the lame.

He who came to breathe eternal life into a valley of dry, dead souls also breathed life into a widow's son, raising him up once more (see Luke 7:11–15).

It was not one or the other—it was both, and both for the glory of God.

In John 20:30–31 we are told, "Many other signs truly did Jesus in the presence of his disciples ... that they might believe that Jesus is the Christ, the Son of God; and that believing you might have life through his name."

The gospel shows that it was the sick, the demon possessed, the hungry, and the poor who came to Jesus and whose lives were changed by His healing touch. Jesus Himself declared that He had come to preach the good news to the poor, the prisoners, the blind, and the oppressed (see Luke 4:18).

Our spirits, which are eternal and infinitely more precious than the whole physical world, are contained in perishable, physical bodies. And throughout the scripture, we see that God used the felt needs of the body to draw people to Himself.

Through the many who were healed from horrible diseases and set free from bondage, Jesus showed Himself as the only one able to save their souls from sin and death.

The mercy ministries Jesus did were not an end in themselves but were rather a means. And it is the same today.

Revolution in World Missions, 117–18
K. P. Yohanna

Jesus' miracles were not so much violation of the natural order, but a restoration of the natural order. God did not create a world with blindness, leprosy, hunger, and death in it. Jesus' miracles were signs that someday all these corruptions of His creation would be abolished.

The Prodigal God, 112
Timothy Keller

What people often forget is that if Jesus created the world (see Genesis 1:1; John 1:3; Colossians 1:15-17), not only are miracles possible, but miracles are actual, because the biggest miracle has already happened-making something out of nothing.

Norman Geisler

Bible miracles are never for mere exploitation or for personal profit to the one who performs the miracle. They are for the good of others. The blind and deaf and lame are healed. The sick and dead are raised. Lepers are cured and sins forgiven. Moreover, those who perform the miracles claim no power of their own but attribute it all to God and only perform the miracle so God may be exalted.

J.B. Tidell

A couple of years ago, I was having breakfast with my niece, Lucy, and my oldest sister, Gladys. These breakfast meetings don't happen as often as they should but at least they do, and we always wind up talking about the Lord and the church.

My niece, my sister, and I all serve the Lord and are members of different churches. We have good and sometimes some not-so-good conversations about issues facing the church and society today. As always, there are some things that come up during our time together that strike a chord with each of us, and this time it was the issue of miracles in the church (body of Christ). Lucy asked, "Where are the miracles?" She did not know that I had already contemplated a book on this subject. I listened and after a while we were all talking about the things we had seen in the past how these events affected us and those in the meeting.

We all had some experience at one point with miracles and thought that at this time, for whatever reason, there was a void. Something is missing. We agreed that there was no lack with the Lord, for we know that God is a miracle-working God. The questions that followed went something like this: Is it that we are not praying enough? Maybe it's because we now have more hope in modern technology than in the Lord. Perhaps there is not enough preaching on the subject of miracles. At the end, we all agreed that we would pray for more in the area of miracles. Our desire is to see people healed and released from their suffering and at the same time to see God glorified and exalted for His mighty working power.

Needless to say, after this meeting I felt that it was time to go ahead with this book. And here we are. So I can say thanks to those breakfast meetings and to the passion my sister and niece have for the Lord and His church. They are committed to prayer, and they seek God every day, interceding for our family and others they have heard of who are in need. I often wonder how many people have received a miracle as a result of my sister and niece faithfully praying for them behind the scenes. They have a gift of intercession, and it is comforting to know that God has people like this all over the world.

I will, for the purpose of this book, concentrate on the stories in the Bible and personal testimonies of people who positioned themselves to receive miracles, and as a result of their actions and God's grace had their needs met. These are the stories that will make up most of this book.

At this time, I am concentrating on the miracles Jesus performed and some of the circumstances surrounding these events. I know there are miracles all throughout the Old Testament and that many miracles took place in the New Testament at the hands of the disciples. That will be the subject of future consideration.

1

Positioning Yourself for a Miracle

Today it seems as if miracles have become a part of the past. We don't hear of many miracles, and it seems like people—even some in the Christian community—have stopped believing, expecting, or even waiting for a miracle. As a result, I have heard Christians and others asking the same question: Where are the miracles? This question reminds me of the story of Gideon. In Judges 6:13, Gideon asks the same question some are asking today, with the same attitude: "If the LORD is with us ... where are all His miracles which our fathers told us about?" This question led me to the task at hand.

I was meditating on the church and its needs when my thoughts turned to the individual needs of people I know; I also thought about the sick and the poor. I thought, *Lord, we need miracles. We need some major miracles.* I realized that some people and some situations are not going to get better without what I call heavenly intervention (miracles).

Then my thoughts turned to some of the people in the Bible who had experienced miracles. I realized that some of the notable miracles happened to people who were looking, hoping, and waiting for them. As a result of their expectation, a good number of people prepared or positioned themselves for the possibility of a miracle.

Some confessed that they would receive a miracle, some prayed to receive a miracle, and some took steps to do something about their situation, like trying to be at the right place at the right time. Humbling themselves and even overcoming personal and public circumstances, they did what they thought needed to be done to receive their miracles. The Bible says, "Faith without works is dead" (James 2:26). We can confess, we can pray, and sometimes we must simply position ourselves to receive a miracle.

I understand that there are those who did nothing and were not expecting anything from God, and yet they received miracles. I believe this to be a demonstration of God's great mercy—a sign to point people to God and His amazing grace.

Miracles are a sign according to John 2:11: "This beginning of His signs Jesus did in Cana of Galilee, and manifested His glory, and His disciples believed in Him."

These miraculous signs help people believe in Jesus, as it states in John 5:36: "But the testimony which I have is greater than the testimony of John; for the works which the Father has given Me to accomplish—the very works that I do—testify about Me, that the Father has sent Me."

On the other hand, I know there are those who have positioned themselves, taken the right steps, made the right confessions, and put their faith in God and yet did not receive answers or miracles. There are things we don't understand, and we have to trust and work with what we know about God.

Remember: God is sovereign—meaning that He is the sole supreme ruler of the universe and nothing is outside of His control. The Lord does whatever pleases Him, in the heavens and on the earth. With God there are no accidents or surprises. He writes all of the world's history and works out everything in conformity with the purpose of His will. God needs no advice or consent for anything He chooses to do. Nor can anyone prevent Him from doing what He pleases. No one can hold back His hand or say to Him, "What have You done?"[1]

We cannot control, manipulate, use, persuade, or trick God into doing anything for us. He is God, and if we could by our actions (or anything else) make Him do something, then we would lose the sense of awe in our relationship with the Almighty—and He would not be worthy of our worship.

In the book of James it says that we should call the elders of the church to pray for the sick. James 5:13–15[13] says:

> Is anyone among you suffering? *Then* he must pray. Is anyone cheerful? He is to sing praises. Is anyone among you sick? *Then* he must call for the elders of the church and they are to pray over him, anointing him with oil in the name of the Lord; and the prayer offered in faith will restore the one who is sick, and the Lord will raise him up, and if he has committed sins, they will be forgiven him.

Notice the words above: "Is anyone suffering? Then he must pray." The question is, pray for what? The answer is to pray for healing.

---

[1] From the book *Ultimate Questions* by John Blanchards (Evangelical Press, 1987). The sovereignty of God is a major study, and it will be impossible to discuss here. For future study, read *Suffering and the Sovereignty of God* by John Piper and Justin Taylor (Crossway Books and Bibles).

Then notice the words that follow: "Is anyone among you sick? Then he must call for the elders of the church, and they are to pray over him, anointing him with oil in the name of the Lord; and the prayer offered in faith will restore the one who is sick, and the Lord will raise him up." This to me is a way of positioning yourself. Are you suffering? You must pray. Are you sick? You must call the elders of the church. These are the things you must do if you want to receive a miracle.

I pray that this book will provoke and encourage you to position yourself and others for miracles because I believe that in many ways we have not positioned ourselves or others for miracles.

The Bible teaches us that God is the same yesterday, today, and forever, and like Mahalia Jackson used to sing, "It is no secret what God can do. What He's done for others He can do for you."

Read the following pages prayerfully, and let these stories bring you to a place of faith and hope in God and His word. Maybe you do not have a need for a miracle in your life right now—and be thankful that you don't—but don't forget the needs of others. Maybe you can use your faith for others who are in need of a miracle. Robert C. Chapman said the following about intercession: "It is well for a child of God to pray for himself, but a more excellent thing is to pray for others. God honors the spirit of intercession."[2]

---

[2] Robert L Peterson and Alexander Strauch, *Agape Leadership: Lessons in Spiritual Leadership from the Life of R. C. Chapman*, 77.

2

Reasons Why Some May Not Receive Miracles

There are many reasons why people may not receive a miracle, and the following are a few examples.

1. Lack of Knowledge

Hosea 4:6 says, "My people are destroyed for lack of knowledge."

This is a major reason why some do not experience the power of God in the area of miracles—they simply do not know. There is no knowledge of God's will to heal and do miracles. If you take the time to look at the word of God, you will see healings and miracles throughout the Old and New Testaments. The Bible is the word of God, and it reveals to us the will of God. All these miracles and healings are not just signs of His love and power; they are a declaration of His will for humankind. He never changes. You need to know this: if He never changes, then His will is the same today as it was yesterday. Hebrews 13:8 says, "Jesus Christ is the same yesterday and today and forever."

2. Lack of Faith

If you lack knowledge, then it is hard to have faith. Therefore, we need to expose people to the word of God. If you don't have faith, please keep on reading and take a good look at what the word of God has to say. Romans 10:17 states, "So faith comes from hearing, and hearing by the word of Christ" (reading is a sort of hearing). This teaches me that faith comes from the word of Christ. Because faith comes from the word of Christ, faith can be nurtured through God's word; the more you read, the more your faith will be increased.

Faith for miracles must have a foundation, and that foundation is not just faith in itself; it is the faith inspired through and by the word of God. By reading the accounts in the word of God, you will grow in faith for miracles. Mark 9:23 says, "And Jesus said to him, 'If You can?' All things are possible to him who believes."

3. Misplaced Faith

Your faith should be in God and His word—not in a person or in a religion. Religion does not save or heal. People do not save or heal. They are only vessels God uses like He used Peter and Paul or your pastor. Don't sit around waiting for the next big evangelist to come to town. Your faith should be in the Lord, and it should be in whomever He chooses to use.

Remember: it is the Lord who does the miracle. Acts 3:1–14 puts this in context when Peter and John healed the lame man at the Beautiful Gate and the people were amazed and wondered about this miracle. Peter said in Acts 3:12, "Men of Israel, why are you amazed at this, or why do you gaze at us, as if by our own power or piety we had made him walk?" In the next verse, Peter tells them who did this and who they should praise and worship. He points to "the God of Abraham, Isaac and Jacob, the God of our fathers, has glorified His servant Jesus" (v. 13). There it is: "His servant Jesus." Our gaze should be on the Lord Jesus Christ—not on other people. Put your faith in Jesus. All the glory and praise belongs to the Lord. Not to your faith, not to your pastor, and not to your religion or your church—but to the Lord.

Calvin also warned against false miracles:

> When we hear that (miracles) were appointed only to seal the truth, shall we employ them to confirm falsehoods? In the first place, it is right to investigate and examine that doctrine which, as the Evangelist says, is superior to miracles. Then, if it is approved, it may rightly be confirmed from miracles. Yet, if one does not tend to seek men's glory but God's (John 7:18; 8:50), this is a mark of true doctrine, as Christ says. Since Christ affirms this test of doctrine, miracles are wrongly valued that are applied to any other purpose than to glorify the name of the one God (Deut. 13:12).[3]

4. Disqualifying Themselves

The issue will almost always be worthiness. "I am not worthy" is what I hear people say. As far as I can see, worthiness has never been a requirement for a miracle. If worthiness was a requirement for a miracle, we would all be in trouble. Can you imagine trying to become worthy while you are in such a great need? Look at the scriptures and see how Jesus dealt with people who were not worthy.

---

[3] John Calvin, "Prefatory Address to King Francis," in *The Institutes of the Christian Religion*, ed. John T. McNeill, trans. Ford Lewis Battles, (Philadelphia: Westminster, 1960), 17.

When Jesus went to heal Jairus's daughter He did not inquire as to her worthiness, or Jairus's worthiness (Mark 5:21–23). Jesus just went with Jairus to heal his daughter. We should also remember that salvation had nothing to do with our worthiness, and miracles have nothing to do with whether we are worthy or not. In fact, just like salvation, we were not worthy, but we received it from the Lord as a gift, "For the wages of sin is death, but the free gift of God is eternal life in Christ Jesus our Lord" (Romans 6:23). Miracles are the same in that this is the grace of God in operation toward man and his needs.

5. **Try to Buy**

When Jesus sent out His disciples to preach the gospel of the kingdom this is part of what He said,

> "And as you go, preach, saying, 'The kingdom of heaven is at hand.' Heal *the* sick, raise *the* dead, cleanse *the* lepers, cast out demons. Freely you received, freely give. Do not acquire gold, or silver, or copper for your money belts." (Matthew 10:7–9)

If anyone says you must pay or join some group to be eligible to receive a miracle, you are being misled. Once again you should look at the scriptures and see if God ever charged anyone for a miracle. You don't have to give money, bring food, clean the church, or make promises. When it comes to miracles, you do not have to bargain with God. Miracles are a free gift from God the Father to you. The Bible says in James 1:17, "Every good thing given and every perfect gift is from above, coming down from the Father of lights, with whom there is no variation or shifting shadow."

After you have received a miracle, should you show your gratitude? Yes. Be thankful. Give praise to God. Acknowledge the fact that it was the Lord through His mercy and grace who delivered you from your situation. Find a way to express your gratitude to the Lord. Change your ways. Tell others all about what Jesus has done for you. Like Jesus said to some who had received a miracle, "Go and sin no more" (John 5:1–15). In the gospel of Luke 17:11–20 you will find ten lepers who came to Jesus asking for healing, and the miracle was that He healed all of them at once. Now among these ten lepers, there was only one who had enough humility and thankfulness in his heart to come back and glorify God with a loud voice. Out of ten, only one came back to express his gratitude. I believe the story of this great healing speaks to the issue of thankfulness. We should take this person's example when it comes to showing our gratitude.

6. **No Relationship with Christ**

Some people think that because they don't have a relationship with the Lord now, they can't receive mercy from Him. What they don't know is that not everyone who received a miracle in the Old and New Testament were related to God or His people.

I think that sometimes we make the mistake of trying to get people into a relationship with God before we pray for them. We should pray for them and let God do what He does best when it comes to healing and performing miracles. It may be easier to lead a person into a relationship with Jesus after he or she has received a healing or miracle!

Some of the miracles I have witnessed or have been a part of happened to people who had no relationship with Jesus or His church. This reveals the great of God's mercy. The Bible says that

God is rich in mercy, "But God, being rich in mercy, because of His great love with which He loved us" (Ephesians 2:4).

7. Failure to Discern Who Jesus Is

It is hard to believe Jesus for a miracle if you don't know who He really is. Matthew 13:54–58 states:

> He came to His hometown and began teaching them in their synagogue, so that they were astonished, and said, "Where did this man get this wisdom and these miraculous powers? Is not this the carpenter's son? Is not His mother called Mary, and His brothers, James and Joseph and Simon and Judas? And His sisters, are they not all with us? Where then did this man get all these things?" And they took offense at Him but Jesus said to them, "A prophet is not without honor except in his hometown and in his own household." And He did not do many miracles there because of their unbelief.

These folks had heard His teaching. They were astonished by His wisdom and miraculous powers, which imply that they had seen or witnessed some kind of miracle. But they could only see Jesus through their natural eyes and referred to Him only in human terms, like these, "This man," "the carpenter's son," and "whose mother is Mary."

They did not discern that Jesus was the Son of God who had power and authority to do these things. As a result, they did not have enough faith in Him for themselves. Their lack of faith was based on their inability to receive Jesus for who He really is. And the text says, He did not do many miracles there because of *"their unbelief"* (Mark 13:38). They failed to discern beyond the natural and therefore could not receive. How sad! Jesus was there, ready, willing, and able, and they did not position themselves for miracles.

8. The Wrong Attitude and Motive

A few years ago, we had an evangelist coming to our church to preach. He had a notable ministry of praying for the sick and the sick would recover. I knew of a young man in our neighborhood who had been shot and was crippled as a result. He had lost the ability to use his legs and was bound to a wheelchair. I went to invite this young man to our Sunday meeting, so he would be able to hear the word of God, receive prayer, and possibly receive a miracle.

After I introduced myself, I invited him to the meeting. He asked me where the service was and what time it would start. When I told him the time, he said he could not come to the meeting because it was at the same time as the Chicago Bulls basketball game.

Needless to say, I was shocked. I could not believe my ears. Here we were offering him the possibility to walk again, to be delivered from the bondage of a wheelchair, but the Bulls game came first.

Well, he ended up getting a friend to record the game for him, and he came to the meeting but was not healed. I think it had something to do with his priorities.

James 4:3 says, "You ask and do not receive, because you ask with wrong motives, so that you may spend *it* on your pleasures." The Reformed Study Bible says this on James 4:3: "God refuses to grant our petitions when they proceed from evil desires." To pray from wrong motives is not to pray in faith.

9. Some People Choose Death Instead of Life

Unfortunately, some people have a death wish. For reasons unknown, some people would rather die. Some are depressed, while others are just tired of their situation. They are tired of fighting and maybe tired of hoping. Others want to join their loved ones who have gone on before them.

They believe that death is the best way out for them and therefore sometimes welcome disease and refuse healing prayer. I know this is an unpopular topic to address, but this even exists among believers. They have no motivation or even a desire to position themselves for a miracle. Therefore trying to intercede for them like Jairus did for his daughter might not work.

Sometimes before I pray for people, I ask them, "What do you want?" I may have been summoned to a hospital by the wishes of others and not the patient. This is a good time to pray, "Lord, Your will be done."

Why would people want to die?

The reasons are too many to mention, but here are a few.

The first is sin. When people are in the midst of sin or have some gross hidden sin in their lives, they may get to the place where they believe it would be better to die. As a result, they might ignore their health and sometimes don't care for a miracle.

You may recall that when Jesus came to Peter, he said, "Go away from me Lord, for I am a sinful man!" (Luke 5:8). It wouldn't be much of a stretch to say that this is like people who believe they are too sinful or that their particular sin excludes them from forgiveness or in this case from a healing, or a miracle. Don't forget that many times Jesus forgave the sin first and then performed a miracle. See Mark 2:1–12 and specifically verse 5.

After Satan has tempted people to sin or violate God's word and compromise their life and testimony, he then works on their guilt and emotions to make them feel so unworthy that they just want to die. He wants to take their lives, and they think it's just their own thoughts and emotions. Listen to what Jesus says about Satan in John 10:10: "The thief comes only to steal and kill and destroy."

Satan is referred to as a thief, a destroyer, and a murderer. He will steal your joy and destroy your life, and if you let him, he will take your life.

People in this situation want to punish themselves and think that death is what they deserve. Some even believe that this is the best way to avoid shame and disgrace to their family and so they would even turn away the Lord and all He has for them.

I would encourage them to hold on to the Lord. He still loves them, He still forgives sin, and He still heals and performs miracles. The fact is that most of the people I will write about in the following pages were not worthy and yet they received from the Lord mercy (unmerited favor) and were healed.

As a result of these healings and miracles, most of these people drew closer to God and became more faithful than before. In addition, their stories became part of the story of man's redemption and an encouragement to a multitude to come to Christ.

10. Chronic and Long-Term Condition

Some people have been suffering with long-term conditions since they were children or for so many years that they have gotten used to this situation and perhaps feel it may be too late. Why bother now? Well, if you look at the miracle ministry of Jesus in the Bible, you will see that long-term conditions and chronic situations did not stop Jesus from helping people get set free. See Luke 13:10–13. This woman had been sick for eighteen years, and Jesus set her free. Look at John 5:1–17. This man was in this condition for thirty-eight years. It is never too late for you to receive a miracle. Jesus is not put off by the length of your illness or condition.

11. Settling for Less Than God Wants

Once at a church meeting when I went to pray for a man who was in the line of prayer. I asked him if he needed a healing, and he said his knees were bad. So I offered to pray for him, and he stopped me.

I asked him, "What's wrong?"

His reply shocked me. He said, "If I get healed then I can't collect my disability payments and I will have to go back to work."

Well, I could not understand this kind of thinking and left him behind because he had settled for less than God wanted for him.

The disability issue has come up at several meetings over a course of time. I mean, people not wanting to be healed because they would then have to go back to work! I have to admit that this caught me by surprise, and it disappointed me to see that people were willing to stay in their condition, suffering needlessly and continuously, just for a paycheck that they did not or would not work for.

As a result, they have become a burden to their families, friends, the community and even the taxpayers. I wonder what God thinks of this. Please don't settle for less than God's best.

I know that this is not true of everyone who is on disability. There are people both young and old who are disabled for many reasons. I believe that most people would rather be healed and be as productive and as creative as ever.

There are people who want so badly to return to the workforce and provide for their families with their labor, but they just can't because of their situation. To them I say be encouraged. God can provide for your needs even through your disability.

Your disability check can in fact be your miracle provision from God. I have traveled to other countries where there are almost no governmental provisions made for the disabled. People suffer not only from their disabilities but from the fact that they cannot provide for their families.

As you can see, there are many reasons why some people will not receive a miracle. It has nothing to do with your worthiness or the amount of money you give or don't give. It's not the person praying for you or the denomination you are a part of. It is all because of what God has done for us at the cross through Jesus Christ.

Don't be discouraged! Even if the condition is chronic, hereditary, accidental, environmental, or self-inflicted, God is able, willing, and ready to help you.

When it comes to a miracle or a healing, please do not dismiss your doctor's orders. Even if you feel better, always make sure you stay on your medications until your doctor or medical professional can confirm your healing or miracle. Don't skip your medical appointments. Don't stop your treatments. People with diabetes, high blood pressure, and other conditions who are healed miraculously can only have their healing confirmed with proper medical testing. Please know that a genuine miracle from the Lord will survive the scrutiny of a medical professional and a medical test.

Listen to the words of Charles Spurgeon, who himself often used medicines to deal with some of his infirmities.

> It would not be wise to live by a supposed faith, and cast off the physician and his medicines, any more than to discharge the butcher, and the tailor, and expect to be fed and clothed by faith.
>
> We make use of medicine, but these can do nothing apart from the Lord, "who healeth all our diseases."
>
> Charles Spurgeon on Medicine
>
> Beloved and yet Afflicted
>
> Sermon 1518

What follows are the stories of people like you and me. They are mostly from the Bible, and because of that, we tend to read them like things that happened long ago to special people who just so happened to be around during the earthly ministry of Jesus and His apostles. Remember that Jesus is just as present today as He was then and that we are not that different from the people you are going to read about. I have included a couple of my own personal stories and experiences only to demonstrate that God meets the needs of ordinary people, and He can and does use ordinary people when it comes to miracles. All the glory is His.

If you do not know Christ as your Savior and Lord, this would be a good time to open your heart to Jesus and ask Him to forgive you of your sins and heal your soul so you can have a relationship with Him. The greatest miracle of all is the forgiveness of your sins.

A physical healing will only last for a while because it is appointed unto man once to die and then comes the judgment. The healing of your soul through Christ's forgiveness of your sins will last forever.

This is the day of salvation.

You may have picked up this book because you need a miracle. I hope that God will use this work to encourage your faith for a miracle, but the most important miracle of all is the forgiveness of your sin and the salvation of your soul. For that to take place, all you need to do is acknowledge that you are a sinner and that the only one who can save you from your sin is the Lord Jesus Christ.

Take this time to ask Him for forgiveness and receive the free gift of God, which is eternal life. "For God so loved the world, that He gave His only begotten Son, that whoever believes in Him shall not perish, but have eternal life" (John 3:16). This is the miracle that will last forever. I encourage you to open your heart and surrender your life to Him today.

3

Healing of a Nobleman's Son

Therefore He came again to Cana of Galilee where He had made the water wine And there was a royal official whose son was sick at Capernaum. When he heard that Jesus had come out of Judea into Galilee, he went to Him and was imploring Him to come down and heal his son; for he was at the point of death. So Jesus said to him, "Unless you people see signs and wonders, you simply will not believe." The royal official said to Him, "Sir, come down before my child dies." Jesus said to him, "Go; your son lives." The man believed the word that Jesus spoke to him and started off. As he was now going down, his slaves met him, saying that his son was living. So he inquired of them the hour when he began to get better. Then they said to him, "Yesterday at the seventh hour the fever left him." So the father knew that it was at that hour in which Jesus said to him, "Your son lives"; and he himself believed and his whole household. This is again a second sign that Jesus performed when He had come out of Judea into Galilee." (John 4:46–54)

This is a beautiful story of a man who was desperately seeking a miracle for his son. I can assume that being a royal official he may have had benefits and perhaps access to whatever medical help was available at this time. Yet his son was not healed. In fact, his son was now at the point of death and only a miracle could save him.

This royal official went beyond himself. He positioned himself to receive a miracle by traveling at least a day's journey away to find Jesus in Galilee and implore Him to return with him back home to heal his son.

I believe that the reason why this man went to look for Jesus in Cana of Galilee is because Jesus had a reputation here of performing miracles. John 4:46 says, "He came again to Cana of Galilee where He had made water wine."

I don't know what, if anything, else this man had heard about Jesus, but this was apparently enough to motivate him to seek Jesus.

> There was a royal official whose son was sick at
> Capernaum. When he heard that Jesus had come
> out of Judea into Galilee, he went to Him and was
> imploring Him to come down and heal his son;
> for he was at the point of death. (John 4:46–47)

Being a "royal official," this man humbled himself and took this journey, not knowing if he would ever see his son alive again. Sometimes we put more importance in being with our loved ones when they are sick or suffering, rather than reaching out to Jesus on their behalf.

This man went to find Jesus, not knowing if Jesus would even give him the time of day. You see, there is no sign of a previous relationship with the Lord, and his plea to the Lord was simple. We should also notice that he did not offer to pay or give anything in return. He simply said, "Sir, come down before my child dies."

Jesus said to him, "Go; your son lives." And as the story goes, the man believed the word that Jesus spoke to him.

The Bible tells us that while the man was yet a distance from his home his slaves met him with the good news "Your son lives!" Can you imagine the joy in his heart when he heard those words? Well, even though he was celebrating the good news, he also verified with his slaves the hour his son got healed and reasoned that it was the same hour that Jesus had given the word to him that his son lives.

This royal official took the following steps:

- He did not consider his own reputation as a royal official.
- He took the long journey, not knowing if he would see his son alive again.
- He went looking for Jesus—not anyone else.
- He recognized the urgency and hopelessness of his situation because his son was at the point of death.
- He had no assurances as to the Lord's reaction to his need. This was a situation where his title and position had no influence.
- He humbled himself by imploring.

This man positioned himself for this miracle. He went beyond himself. Will you? What will you do?

Remember, he had no guarantee. But he still went to look for Jesus. What I am pointing out is that he did something. He moved. He asked. He believed the word of the Lord. Jesus did not turn him down.

After the healing of his son, it is recorded that he and his family believed. So the miracle was not just a healing of a son but the salvation of a whole family. I believe this was a bigger miracle than just the healing of his son.

Don't just sit there with your need. Do something! Look for the Lord. Find Him and get ready to believe and receive.

1. Don't accept your situation.
2. Don't give up.
3. Don't let go of the hope.
4. Don't stop believing.
5. Don't stop looking.
6. Don't stop asking.
7. Don't stop expecting.
8. Don't stop knocking.
9. Don't stop dreaming.

God is good, and His mercies endure forever. "The LORD is good to all, and His mercies are over all His works" (Psalm 145:9).

4

Let Down Your Net and Catch a Miracle

Now it happened that while the crowd was pressing around Him and listening to the word of God, He was standing by the lake of Gennesaret; and He saw two boats lying at the edge of the lake; but the fishermen had gotten out of them and were washing their nets. And He got into one of the boats, which was Simon's, and asked him to put out a little way from the land. And He sat down and began teaching the people from the boat. When He had finished speaking, He said to Simon, "Put out into the deep water and let down your nets for a catch." Simon answered and said, "Master, we worked hard all night and caught nothing, but I will do as You say and let down the nets." When they had done this, they enclosed a great quantity of fish, and their nets began to break; so they signaled to their partners in the other boat for them to come and help them. And they came and filled both of the boats, so that they began to sink. But when Simon Peter saw that, he fell down at Jesus' feet, saying, "Go away from me Lord, for I am a sinful man!" For amazement had seized him and all his companions because of the catch of fish which they had taken; and so also were James and John, sons of Zebedee, who were partners with Simon. And Jesus said to Simon, "Do not fear, from now on you will be catching men." When they had brought their boats to land, they left everything and followed Him. (Luke 5:1–11)

I know there are times when we need a miracle and it's not related to a physical healing. Sometimes we need miracles for our finances, our business, or our marriage and nothing short of a miracle will save us or keep us from loss.

For those with other needs that are not physical in nature, but still require heavenly intervention, I have good news Jesus can help you receive a miracle. But like those who needed a physical miracle, you need to position yourself according to the word and will of God.

The men in this story were fishing all night long. They were seasoned fishermen who knew their trade. They knew where, when, and how to fish. They were professionals. Even though they had the ability, knowledge, and equipment (boats and nets) and worked all night, they caught nothing. As a result, they were ready to give up. In fact, they had quit and were washing their nets, getting ready to go home empty-handed, accepting the fact that there was nothing else they could do to change the present results.

Imagine how this felt. They were working hard all night long. They had the right tools. They were at what they thought was the right place at the right time, doing what they do best, and things didn't work out the way they thought it would. Their faith was in their own experience, ability, and equipment.

Well it may not be time to give up. Simon and the others had given up. They came to the end of their own ability and wisdom, but praise God, Jesus showed up. When Jesus shows up, the situation will change. He asked them to reposition themselves, to go out again, and this time to go deeper. "Put out into the deep water and let down your nets for a catch" (Luke 5:4).

I am glad that Jesus didn't listen to Simon, because Simon was like some of us. We hear or read the word of God and know that God is speaking to us and giving us instructions, yet we try to explain to God what we have already done, how long we have been at it, and how tired we are of doing these things.

We are telling God the reasons why we don't want to go on. It is good to know that sometimes God does not pay attention to our whining. Jesus told them to go out a little bit farther into the deep (reposition) and try again. Don't give up!

To Simon and the others, this did not seem like the thing to do. You see, Jesus was the son of a carpenter, not the son of a fisherman. While I don't know how much experience Jesus had with the fishing industry, I do know that these men had plenty of experience. And now they were receiving instructions from Jesus (a carpenter) to go at it again.

The good thing is that they finally listened. Even though it did not make sense to them, they went out to the deep waters and let down their nets. As a result, maybe without realizing it, Simon positioned himself for probably the greatest catch they had ever made. It was a miraculous catch, one so big that their nets began to break and it almost sank their boats.

Sometimes receiving a miracle can be that simple. Just do what Jesus says to do. You reposition yourself by obeying the word of the Lord. Again our faith should not be in our own ability, training, knowledge, equipment, or experience. It should be in the Lord and what He has asked us to do. We need to understand that He has resources we know nothing of. He even knows where the fish are. "Let us not lose heart in doing good, for in due time we will reap if we do not grow weary" (Galatians 6:9).

5

Peter's Mother-In-Law Healed

And immediately after they came out of the synagogue, they came into the house of Simon and Andrew, with James and John. Now Simon's mother-in-law was lying sick with a fever; and immediately they spoke to Jesus about her. And He came to her and raised her up, taking her by the hand, and the fever left her, and she waited on them. When evening came, after the sun had set, they began bringing to Him all who were ill and those who were demon-possessed. And the whole city had gathered at the door. And He healed many who were ill with various diseases, and cast out many demons; and He was not permitting the demons to speak, because they knew who He was. (Mark 1:29–34)

What we have recorded here is a healing that takes place at Simon's house. Simon was a disciple of Jesus's. The person who received the healing was Simon's mother-in-law. We find that a crowd came from the surrounding area, and here I believe was a mix of those who were believers and those who were not. Yet many in this crowd received healings and miracles.

In the first case, Jesus arrived at Simon and Andrew's house and found that Simon's mother-in-law was sick. She was in bed with a fever (v. 30). As Charles Spurgeon puts it, "Into Simon's house sickness had entered; fever in a deadly form had prostrated his mother-in-law."[4] The fever was severe. Now in the same verse we see that the way they positioned themselves was by speaking to Jesus about her illness, we may call this intercession, or to plead the case for another.

There are times when people cannot speak for themselves. Maybe they are afraid and just don't know how to ask? Perhaps they don't have the ability? In this case someone else needs to step in like the royal official in chapter 3 of this book. His son could not go to Jesus, but the royal official went on behalf of his son.

The fact is, Jesus was there, Simon's mother-in-law was there, and wherever Jesus is, there is an opportunity for a healing or a miracle, even if it's just a fever. Sometimes we position ourselves by asking or interceding for someone else. The disciples took the opportunity before them and asked Jesus to heal her. You see, sometimes people don't speak up. They don't ask.

It's amazing to think that sometimes we suffer because we don't ask for help. The Bible says, "Ask, and it will be given to you; seek, and you will find; knock, and it will be opened to you" (Matthew 7:7)

I remember when a young boy came up to me after a meeting where I had just finished preaching and asked me if I would pray for his mother. He did not want his mother to go back home in her condition. She was in the meeting and did not ask for herself. She was ready to go home in this situation, but thank God for

---

[4] *Morning and Evening* by Charles H. Spurgeon (1834-1892). © September 26, 2003 Good News/Crossway Books

this young boy who wanted his mother healed (out of the mouth of babes).

The women would have left the same way she came in. She did not make a move. She did not go forward for prayer. She did not position herself for a healing. She was going the wrong way. She was going out with her condition to suffer needlessly. But thank God for the faith of a little boy who loved his mother and asked on her behalf. He was interceding for his mom, just like Simon did for his mother-in-law.

Going back to the story of the disciples and Simon's sick mother-in-law, Jesus, after hearing the request from Andrew and Simon, reached out and healed this woman. After she was healed, she got up and served them. Simon asked, and she received. He did not ask for himself; he asked for someone else.

After this healing we find in verse 32 that, "they began bringing to Him (Jesus) all who were ill and those who were demon-possessed." I don't know who is being referred to when it says "they" brought to Him all who were ill; it just says "they." I thank God for those who know how to position others to receive healings, miracles, and deliverance from demons. Jesus responded to the people who were being brought to Him. Mark 1:34 says, "And He healed many who were ill with various diseases, and cast out many demons."

When we position ourselves and in some instances others, we are opened to receive what we asked for. The reason I say some instances is that even here we see that the word of God says "many were healed." It does not say all.

Why weren't they all healed? I don't know, but as I grow in my faith and age, I can deal with these things better. I know that not all get healed. I have lived long enough to know that the Bible declares "it is appointed unto man once to die and then comes the judgment" (Hebrews 9:27).

I remember a lady who came to me and asked me to pray for her mother, who was ill and in the hospital. When I asked her how old her mother was, she said ninety-three years old. Even though I believe it is God's will to heal people, I also know that it is appointed unto man once to die and that we do not all die of natural causes. I prayed for her and carefully asked her to consider her mother's heart (desire). Some people are tired and just want to go home (to heaven).

Our elders are sometimes wiser than we are and are full of faith for their homecoming. My mother would say to me, "I am ready, and I almost can't wait to see my Lord and Savior face to face." My sisters and brothers and I wanted her healed. She wanted to go home.

I too will someday pass away. How? I do not know. My mother died at eighty-seven, and I have come to understand that some people will receive what has been termed as a permanent healing or a deliverance from their suffering.

My daughter-in-law passed away a few years ago from breast cancer. I have to admit my family and I took this very hard. She was young and had two daughters. The youngest was eight years old and the oldest was fourteen at the time. She was thirty-five when she went home to be with the Lord. Before that, we had the great privilege of leading her to faith in Christ, and shortly after that, I baptized her, so we know that she is with the Lord.

The Bible says:

> For this perishable must put on the imperishable, and this mortal must put on immortality. But when this perishable will have put on the imperishable, and this mortal will have put on immortality, then will come about the saying that is written, "Death is swallowed up in victory." O death, where is your victory? O death, where is your sting? (1 Corinthians 15:53–55)

The fact that my daughter-in law was saved, that she gave her heart to the Lord Jesus, took the sting of death and swallowed it up in victory.

Charles Spurgeon once said this:

> We may not make sure that the Lord will at once remove all disease from those we love, but we may know that believing prayer for the sick is far more likely to be followed by restoration than anything else in the world; and where this avails not, we must meekly bow to his will by whom life and death are determined. The tender heart of Jesus waits to hear our grief's let us pour them into his patient ear.[5]

When my family and I lived on Montana Street in Chicago, one of the ladies on our street came to my door and asked if I would be willing to speak to another neighbor at the end of the block because the doctors had just given him three months to live. He had cancer. They knew that I was a Christian and that I was a pastor of a church.

---

[5] 5 Ibid.

I went and knocked on his door, and he answered. I then asked him to come outside so I could speak with him. We sat at his front steps, and I let him know that I was aware of his situation. As we talked, tears ran down his face. I started to speak to him and tried to get him to understand that he would soon have to face the Lord and that he should deal with the issues of his heart.

We talked and talked, and he confessed that he had some bitterness in his heart toward his former employer who had laid him off before retirement. He also had issues with his church (he was Catholic) and its leaders. He was hurt and even angry. After a while I challenged his bitterness and asked him to forgive those who had hurt him and seek to face God with a pure heart and a clean conscience. He agreed, so I then asked him if I could pray with him, and he said yes.

I began to pray for him because I knew he did not know how to pray. While I prayed, he began to cry. The tears flowed as he listened to my prayer. After I prayed, we hugged, and I went home.

Let me tell you about this unsolicited miracle. You see, he did not request this meeting. It was someone else who interceded on his behalf. It was the woman down the street who asked me to go and talk to him. And here is the result of that meeting. Several years later when we were getting ready to move to our new location to work for the Lord, all of our neighbors came to see us off. They sat in our living room, saved and unsaved, young and old, and one by one they started to share with us what we meant to them while we lived in that neighborhood. As we heard these wonderful people share their hearts with us, we were moved to tears. The stories were more then we could handle, and the truth is that we did not even notice all the things that had taken place with these folks. Then it was this man's turn.

At this time he had already outlived the doctor's sentence by more than three years. He said that on the day I prayed for him, he felt better. He went on to say that he had just come from the doctor's office, and the doctor told him that whatever he was doing, he should keep on doing it because he now was healthier than the doctor. This man has not to my knowledge accepted Jesus as Savior, but he is still alive, and I have been out of Chicago for more than seven years.

I have seen great healings at some of our meetings, and yet I have officiated at a lot of funerals. I know from experience that not all get healed, but I will not stop proclaiming the goodness of God and the fact that I still believe in the will of God to heal people. This is not a Pentecostal or Charismatic thing; this is a Bible thing, and it is Jesus in action.

Getting back to our text, you see that people were positioned by their friends for healing and miracles. Make sure that you have some friends who believe and have faith for you in the time of need. At the same time, don't stop looking for opportunities to intercede for others or bring others to the place of blessings and miracles just like Simon did with his mother-in-law.

6

Jesus Cleanses a Leper

> When Jesus came down from the mountain, large
> crowds followed Him. And a leper came to Him
> and bowed down before Him, and said, "Lord, if
> You are willing, You can make me clean." Jesus
> stretched out His hand and touched him, saying,
> "I am willing; be cleansed." And immediately his
> leprosy was cleansed. (Matthew 8:1–3)

In this passage we find a leper who had not given up on the
possibility for a miracle. He did not give up on himself or resign
himself to a life of despair. This man decided to do something
to position himself (by faith) in the presence of Jesus where he
thought he could receive a miracle.

This was a horrible, crippling, and terminal disease, and if that
was not bad enough, it also made people social outcasts. In those
days it was unlawful for this man to be in the midst of a crowd.
You see, this disease was contagious, and those who had it were
considered unclean even by the religious community. Those
who had such diseases were ostracized, kept apart from others,
including their relatives, and were for the most part not allowed

to be near the general public without declaring in a loud voice that they were coming through and were unclean.

This man heard that Jesus had come down from the mountain and that large crowds were following Him. He may have heard about what Jesus had done for others and made a decision to come to Jesus and ask for a miracle.

The leper made his way through the crowd—perhaps declaring his condition out loud. According to Luke's account of this story, and we know that Luke was a doctor, he said that the man was covered with leprosy (Luke 5:12). And if Luke had made this observation, I am sure others could see the same thing. So this man could not conceal his situation. He had to let everyone know and see him in this state.

Some people would rather hide or hope that Jesus would just come to them in private, but this man did not have that luxury. This was a matter of life or death. It was now or never. Even sick people are sometimes bound by pride or worried about how they look or what others will think of them in their condition. Pride can be a hindrance or an obstacle for some when it comes to healings and miracles. Pride can keep us in bondage.

Look at what this man did to position himself for a miracle.

- He put away his pride. He was covered with leprosy and could not conceal his condition.
- He made his way through the crowd and didn't let anyone get in his way.
- He came by faith, not knowing if he would be received or healed.
- He humbled himself before the Lord.
- He asked, "If you are willing, you can make me clean."

Then the miracle took place: "Jesus stretched out His hand and touched him and said the words, 'I am willing,' and immediately his leprosy was gone." Jesus not only touched the untouchable with his own hand, but he also declared that He was willing to heal the man. Jesus touching this man shows us that God is not put off by our condition. He touched a man with a contagious disease even though others ran or stayed away. Jesus drew near and reached out to him.

Don't give up on yourself. Your situation may seem untouchable to others but not to Jesus, and I hope you hear those eternal words from the Lord, "I am willing." He is willing to reach out and cause you to be immediately healed. I know that healings and miracles don't always happen immediately, but I love that word and several times in His ministry people were healed immediately.

You are not out of reach. Do you think Jesus came down from that mountain to that place by accident? I don't! I believe that Jesus came to the right place at the right time.

There is a song that goes like this:

Shackled by a heavy burden
Neath a load of guilt and shame
Then the hand of Jesus touched me
And now I am no longer the same
He touched me, oh he touched me
And oh the joy that floods my soul
Something happened and now I know
He touched me and made me whole.
Artist: Gaither Vocal Band
Album: Reunion Volume One

7

The Paralytic Healed

When He had come back to Capernaum several days afterward, it was heard that He was at home. And many were gathered together, so that there was no longer room, not even near the door; and He was speaking the word to them. And they came, bringing to Him a paralytic, carried by four men. Being unable to get to Him because of the crowd, they removed the roof above Him; and when they had dug an opening, they let down the pallet on which the paralytic was lying. And Jesus seeing their faith said to the paralytic, "Son, your sins are forgiven." But some of the scribes were sitting there and reasoning in their hearts, "Why does this man speak that way? He is blaspheming; who can forgive sins but God alone?" Immediately Jesus, aware in His spirit that they were reasoning that way within themselves, said to them, "Why are you reasoning about these things in your hearts? "Which is easier, to say to the paralytic, 'Your sins are forgiven'; or to say, 'Get up, and pick up your pallet and walk'? "But so that you may know that the Son of Man has authority on earth to forgive sins"—He said to the paralytic, "I say to you, get up, pick up your pallet and go home." And he got up and immediately picked up the pallet and went out in the sight of everyone, so that they were all amazed and were glorifying God, saying, "We have never seen anything like this." (Mark 2:1–12)

In this passage, Jesus had just come back from ministry to Capernaum, and people in town heard He was back. As a result, a large crowd began to gather at His home. In fact, the crowd was so large that there was no room, not even by the door.

Four men came, bringing with them a paralytic. Because of the crowd, they were unable to get to Jesus. They decided to overcome their circumstances by hoisting this paralytic up to the roof of the house. Then, after creating an opening in the roof, they lowered the paralytic into the house and into the presence of Jesus.

We don't know who these men were. The Bible does not give us their names, but what we know of them is that they brought this paralytic to Jesus looking for a miracle. Again, I say it is good to have friends who will do whatever is necessary to get you to Jesus at the right place at the right time.

They could not get through the crowd with this man, so they took a step of faith and made a way where there was none and positioned the paralytic for a miracle. These four men heard that Jesus was in town and made a decision. They positioned the paralytic for the possibility of a miracle. Faith took action. James 2:26 says, "For just as the body without the spirit is dead, so also faith without works is dead."

They acted in faith, and Jesus responded to their faith.[6] Verse 5 says, "And Jesus seeing their faith said to the paralytic, 'Son, your sins are forgiven.'" And verse 11 says, "I say to you get up, pick up your pallet and go home."

They did something with their faith:

- They brought the paralytic with them to see Jesus.
- They refused to be deterred by the crowd.
- They carried him up to the top of the house.
- They removed the roof.
- They dug the hole.
- They let the man down into the presence of Jesus.

Can you imagine the stir this caused? They removed the roof and dug a hole in a house that did not belong to them. Talk about determination and faith!

What happened? They got their miracle. You see, this was not just a miracle for the paralytic; it was a miracle for the four men who brought him to Jesus, because this is a testimony of their faith and determination to position this man for a miracle.

They did what they had to do to have their need met. It is funny that the Bible does not record anything regarding this paralytic man. For example, was it at his request that they brought him?

---

[6] R. A. Cole, *The Gospel According to St. Mark* (Carol Stream, IL: Tyndale New Testament Commentaries, 1983), 65. As usual, the Lord healed only in response to faith. Here scripture does not make clear the attitude of the sick man himself. He, too, may well have had faith, but it may be that he was too conscious of his own sin to have any confidence in thus approaching the Christ. It is simple to assume that the Lord worked the miracle in response to the robust and active faith of the four friends, who brought a helpless comrade and laid him at Jesus' feet. Their faith showed its reality by its very obstinacy and stubbornness in refusing to give up hope.

Was it his idea? Was it even his idea to go up to the roof? Or did he have any faith for this miracle to happen? We know nothing about this man except that he was a paralytic and that he was brought by his friends.

What we do know is related to the four men who brought this man. It seems that they were the ones with the faith as well as the determination to overcome the circumstances for their friend. "And Jesus seeing their faith said to the paralytic, 'Son, your sins are forgiven'" (Mark 2:5). It was their faith that caught the attention of Jesus. Your faith can position others to receive a miracle. I have seen this over and over again. I have seen others bring in the infirm for prayer and have seen people walk away healed.

I remember a revival meeting in Chicago. The place was jam-packed. There was no room left. We were all standing in the crowd when all of a sudden I saw a body being passed through the crowd, just like one of those rock concerts right over the heads of the people. Later I would find out that this man and his sister were on their way to the meeting when he suffered some kind of attack in the car. His sister, instead of taking him to a hospital, decided to make her way to the revival meeting, where she begged some of the people at the door to please get her brother out of the car and into the building and to the front for prayer.

Well, they all pulled together to get this man to the altar for prayer, and here came this body. It looked lifeless as it was passed overhead. When they got him to the altar, the preacher laid his hands on the man and began praying. Within a minute, the man started to respond and became well. This woman had faith for her brother and overcame the circumstances and got her brother to the right place at the right time and received her miracle.

She did not let the crowd stop her from getting her brother to the stage, where prayer and healings were taking place. She asked for the help of complete strangers, overcame her circumstances, and as a result positioned her brother for a miracle.

Was he a believer? I don't know, but she was, and just like these four men, I believe that it was her faith that made it possible for this healing to take place.

With the paralytic, the greatest miracle that took place was not the physical healing it was the forgiveness of his sins. It is easy to get caught up in the faith of the four men and the miracle that the paralytic received, but Jesus saw his real need—the need to have his sin forgiven. To have your sin forgiven is a far greater miracle.

This miracle we can all receive. Ask Jesus to forgive you of your sins right now, and ask Him to come as Lord to your life and you will receive the greatest miracle of all. You will be born again.

8

A Miracle by the Pool

After these things there was a feast of the Jews, and Jesus went up to Jerusalem. Now there is in Jerusalem by the sheep gate a pool, which is called in Hebrew Bethesda, having five porticoes. In these lay a multitude of those who were sick, blind, lame, and withered, [waiting for the moving of the waters; for an angel of the Lord went down at certain seasons into the pool and stirred up the water; whoever then first, after the stirring up of the water, stepped in was made well from whatever disease with which he was afflicted.] A man was there who had been ill for thirty-eight years. When Jesus saw him lying there, and knew that he had already been a long time in that condition, He said to him, "Do you wish to get well?" The sick man answered Him, "Sir, I have no man to put me into the pool when the water is stirred up, but while I am coming, another steps down before me." Jesus said to him, "Get up, pick up your pallet and walk." Immediately the man became well, and picked up his pallet and began to walk. (John 5:1–9)

What a sight at the pool! There they were—the lame, the blind, the sick, and the withered. They could have been anywhere else with family, with friends, or just at home with their sickness and deformities. They could have been crying, complaining, and depressed, but they were not. They were at the pool, waiting for their chance at a miracle. They had positioned themselves by the pool, waiting for an angel to stir the water. You see, these people obviously had only one hope left: a miracle. So there they were. Their hope and faith had already been turned toward heaven.

In the midst of these people was a man who had been ill for thirty-eight years. What was he doing there? He had, like the others, positioned himself for a miracle. I don't know if he would come there every day or if he was a fixture there. What I do know is that on that day, he was positioned at the right place at the right time. And because he was there, he caught the attention of Jesus. What attracted Jesus's attention to this man? I don't know. ("Jesus saw him lying there," v. 6.) What I do know is that the man was at the right place at the right time. He was positioned and waiting.

Jesus saw the man and knew he had been in that condition for a long time. "Do you wish to get well?" He asked. I wonder if this question is still being asked. I believe that Jesus knows our condition. He knows how long we have suffered, and He would probably ask us the same question: "Do you wish to get well?"

This man had an answer. He said in verse 7, "Sir, I have no man to put me into the pool when the water is stirred up, but while I am coming another steps down before me." I wonder how many times he had been pushed out of the way by others. Or how many times he almost made it but was beaten to the water by someone else. Or how many times he may have felt like giving up.

How often did he have to overcome his discouragement? He had no one to help him, no one to pick him up and get him into the pool. Yet, even though he had been beaten to the pool time and time again, he did not stop going there and waiting for a miracle.

Others may get there before you. Learn to rejoice with them, but don't give up trying or positioning yourself for your miracle. Like this man, keep on going to the right place, and today may be the right time.

When we are sick, hurt, in trouble, or in some kind of need, we have choices. We can stay home and mope, hide, cut people off, cry, complain, and allow depression to set in. Sometimes we might even ignore the attempts of others to help us. Or we can do something. We can become proactive and make our way to the pool, or the place of blessing and opportunity, and see what God will do.

Miracles can happen in a church, a car, a hospital, or a park or even by a pool. Don't limit God. Most of Jesus's miracles happened out in the open and in public.

One time, in my early days of pastoral ministry, I received a phone call from one of our friends, Maritza. She was calling because her sister just had surgery and the doctors had performed the wrong surgery on her. Maritza was crying and afraid because the doctor had just told her that her sister was in serious condition and would probably not make it through the night.

At that moment I could not go to the hospital. I had no car, and there was a snowstorm outside. So I did the only thing that I could think of. I asked her if she was calling from the hospital. She said yes. Then I asked her to get the phone near her sister so she could hear my prayer. She did, and then I began to pray. I asked God for mercy and declared the word of God over the situation and proclaimed healing and a miracle for her in the name of Jesus. I said amen and waited for Maritza to come back to the phone. I encouraged her and also prayed with her for peace.

The next day Maritza called again. She was shouting and praising God. When she calmed down, she told me that the prayer worked. Her sister had survived the night and shocked the doctors by getting up and eating some food. They could not believe what had happened. Maritza and her whole family rejoiced and praised God for the miracle they had received through a phone line. Psalm 107:20 says, "He sent His word and healed them." And just like the story in chapter 3 of this book, Jesus gave the word. "Go your son lives," and the nobleman's son was healed (John 4:50).

There is no distance too great for God. In the midst of the crisis, Maritza did not give up. She called for help. She positioned herself for a miracle by picking up the phone and putting it near her sister's ear. You don't have to be in a church building to get a miracle, and sometimes miracles come without the laying on of hands or anointing with oil. We need to just say the word. After all, remember the official's son? Jesus said, "Go, your son lives." He sent His word and the boy lived. "Then they cried out to the LORD in their trouble; He saved them out of their distresses. He sent His word and healed them, and delivered them from their destructions" (Psalm 107:19–20).

I thank God for doctors. I thank God for science. I thank Him for technology, medicine, hospitals, surgical procedures, nurses, and all that's involved in a patient's care. But sometimes we still need a miracle.

9

Healing on the Sabbath

And He was teaching in one of the synagogues on the Sabbath. And there was a woman who for eighteen years had had a sickness caused by a spirit; and she was bent double, and could not straighten up at all. When Jesus saw her, He called her over and said to her, "Woman, you are freed from your sickness." And He laid His hands on her; and immediately she was made erect again and began glorifying God. But the synagogue official, indignant because Jesus had healed on the Sabbath, began saying to the crowd in response, "There are six days in which work should be done; so come during them and get healed, and not on the Sabbath day." But the Lord answered him and said, "You hypocrites, does not each of you on the Sabbath untie his ox or his donkey from the stall and lead him away to water him? "And this woman, a daughter of Abraham as she is, whom Satan has bound for eighteen long years, should she not have been released from this bond on the Sabbath day?" He said this, all His opponents were being humiliated; and the entire crowd was

rejoicing over all the glorious things being done
by Him. (Luke 13:10–16)

Some illnesses and physical conditions are hereditary. Some
conditions are caused by environmental issues, while others are
the results of accidents or even self-inflicted situations. And other
conditions are brought on by spirits. In this portion of scripture,
we find Jesus teaching in one of the synagogues. While He was
teaching, "there was a woman who was bent double, and could
not straighten up" (v. 11).

The interesting thing about this story is that it is being told by
Luke, who was a doctor. Luke said that this woman had a "sickness
caused by a spirit." This is an interesting statement for an educated
man of medicine, yet he pointed out that her condition was of a
spiritual nature, not physical, environmental, or hereditary.

I don't know how Dr. Luke knew this or what led him to that
conclusion. What I do know is that Jesus did not dispute this.
In fact, Jesus took the time to heal this woman. He called her
over and said, "Women, you are freed from your sickness." He
recognized her sickness, but instead of saying, "You are healed,"
He said, "you are freed." Later, when He answered the synagogue
officials in verse 16, He said, "And this women, a daughter of
Abraham as she is, whom Satan has bound for eighteen long years,
should she not have been released?"

Jesus and Luke both recognized that this condition was brought
on by Satan, not heredity or the environment, and was not the
result of an accident. Verse 11 clearly says that this was a "sickness
caused by a spirit." This was not the result of an accident or a birth
defect. It was, as Jesus said, Satan who brought this condition on
this woman.

My conclusion is as follows:

1. Even though this condition was brought on by Satan, Jesus still had the power to release the women from bondage. So even if conditions or illnesses or diseases are the result of a spirit, Satan, or some kind of spiritual nature Jesus can and will heal, set free, release, and restore.

2. This woman, in my opinion, positioned herself for a miracle. I make that statement based on the fact that she was there at the synagogue when Jesus was there. Did she know that Jesus was going to be there? I don't know. What I do know is that she was there at the right place at the right time when she could have been elsewhere. She made her way there and stayed long enough to catch the attention of Doctor Luke and Jesus.

Some may have a difficult time with the subject matter of illnesses being brought upon people by Satan or spirits, but this passage attests to the fact that there are people who suffer with issues that are not natural.

In *The New Faces of Christianity*, author Philip Jenkins puts it this way:

> For the earliest followers of Jesus—and presumably for Jesus himself—healing and exorcism were essential components of his proclamation. In His acts of healing, Jesus was not just curing individuals, but trampling diabolical forces underfoot, and the signs and wonders represented visible and material tokens of Christ's victory over real forces of evil. Leaders of the early church carried on this tradition.

The word *exorcism* is not used to describe anything like what Hollywood perceives this to be. There is no extended battle between the Lord Jesus Christ and these spirits or Satan. Jesus is Lord and has authority over all these things. As Mark 1:33–34 states, "And the whole city had gathered at the door. And He healed many who were ill with various diseases, and cast out many demons; and He was not permitting the demons to speak, because they knew who He was."

There are also people who firmly believe in the power of spirits and are afraid of this power. In many places around the world this is a reality and people need to be and can be, set free.[7] Further on we will see other instances of spiritual (demonic) activity related to illness in the human condition.

No matter what the situation, be it accidental, hereditary, environmental, or spiritual, Jesus is able to deliver us from all these things.

---

[7] *The New Faces of Christianity* published by Oxford University Press, Inc. © 2006 by Philip Jenkins. Jenkins discusses the issue of Good and Evil. In chapter 5, pages 99–100 he says; "Most Northern readers today would label believers in demons and witchcraft irredeemably pre-modern, pre-scientific, and probably preliterate; and such beliefs would cast doubt on believer's claims to an authentic or intelligent religion. Yet the supernatural approach certainly harks back to the ancient roots of Christianity. To read the gospels is to make the intimate acquaintance of demons and demonic forces. Arguing for a social justice approach to Christianity, Jim Wallis rightly points out that excising references to 'the poor' leaves very little of the biblical text intact. But by the same principle, precious little is left of the New Testament after we purge all mentions of angels, demons, and spirits. Short of healing and miraculous cures, the four gospels would be a slim pamphlet indeed." This quote, in the footnote from comes from Jim Wallis *God's Politics* (San Francisco): Harper publishing San Francisco, 2005; Amanda Porterfield, *Healing in the History of Christianity* (New York) Oxford University Press, 2005.

10

Jesus Restores the Centurion's Servant

And when Jesus entered Capernaum, a centurion came to Him, imploring Him, and saying, "Lord, my servant is lying paralyzed at home, fearfully tormented." Jesus said to him, "I will come and heal him." But the centurion said, "Lord, I am not worthy for You to come under my roof, but just say the word, and my servant will be healed. "For I also am a man under authority, with soldiers under me; and I say to this one, 'Go!' and he goes, and to another, 'Come!' and he comes, and to my slave, 'Do this!' and he does it." Now when Jesus heard this, He marveled and said to those who were following, "Truly I say to you, I have not found such great faith with anyone in Israel … And Jesus said to the centurion, "Go; it shall be done for you as you have believed." And the servant was healed that very moment." (Matthew 8:5–10, 13)

Jesus spent a lot of time in Capernaum, and as a result it seems to be the center of miraculous activity. This centurion loved his servant so much that he took it upon himself to intercede for his servant, who was incapacitated, lying paralyzed and fearfully tormented. In Luke's gospel of the same account, it says that the servant was "sick and about to die" (Luke 7:2). Whether he was lying paralyzed and fearfully tormented, or sick and about to die, this servant could not position himself for a miracle. It was going to take the time, energy, and faith of someone else.

In Mark 2:1–10 we read the story of a paralytic who was brought to Jesus by four of his friends. This man, the centurion's servant, obviously could not be moved. Praise God that he had a friend in his master the centurion, who heard that Jesus had come back to town and decided to act on behalf of his servant. The centurion positioned himself to receive a miracle for his servant.

Intersession is to plead the case of another. The royal official in John 4:46–51 came to intercede for his son. This man came to intercede for his friend and servant.

1. He came to Jesus (he did not wait for Jesus to come to him).
2. He implored Jesus on behalf of his servant (he begged).
3. He humbled himself, acknowledging his unworthiness to have such a person like Jesus come into his home. Notice that Jesus never questioned the man's worthiness. Jesus said, "I will come and heal him." It was the centurion who thought of himself as unworthy to have Jesus come to his home.
4. He asked for Jesus to give the word for his servant to be healed. I don't know where the centurion got the idea or the notion that Jesus did this sort of thing, but he knew something about authority and believed that Jesus had that kind of authority to just give a word and the request would be fulfilled. Even Jesus marveled at his faith, and

this led Him to give the word (the order) and the servant was healed.

This is a picture of how we can position ourselves for a miracle by way of interceding for others:

- The centurion loved his servant.
- He demonstrated that love by his actions.
- He went to look for Jesus.
- He begged Jesus for the servant's healing.
- He acknowledged his own unworthiness.
- He trusted the authority of Jesus to just give a word.

He went home believing that it would be just as Jesus said. And as the testimony goes, in verse 13, "And the servant was healed that very moment."

We may not need a miracle, but I am sure we know someone who does. And we, like the centurion, may someday stand in the place of intercession for someone else and ask for the word to be given.

I hope that these stories and testimonials will help us to recapture our faith and hope in the God of miracles and provoke us to action. We may not always get what we want or expect, but we can still be open to the fact that God is the same yesterday, today, and forever.

I have suffered loss and have even had surgery, but I will not throw in the towel. I have seen too much and have taken a good look at the word of God and know that there are still opportunities for miracles.

Speaking of the power of testimonies and miracles, I would like to share a personal experience. Shortly after I came to know the

Lord as Savior, I went to a church where testimonies were always encouraged from the members of the church (it was a part of our service format).

Testimonies do two things: they help the person testifying to express thankfulness and praise to the Lord, and they help to encourage faith in others. One evening, I sat there and heard a woman testify how through her life she had endured much suffering with headaches. These headaches would often incapacitate her and even keep her from being a good mother or employee.

She started seeking the Lord for relief, and one day while she was riding the bus she began to feel the symptoms coming on. At that point she said that she declared healing for herself in the name of the Lord Jesus Christ and decided that she would no longer suffer from these headaches. As her testimony goes, she was freed from these headaches for more than a year and was praising God for her healing.

As I sat there listening to her, my faith was being stirred, and I thought to myself that if God could do this for her then He could do the same for me. This is what testimonies do; they inspire others to trust God. It was at that moment I said, "Lord, please help me and free me from my headaches. At that moment I did not feel anything, but I was determined to trust God."

That was in the spring of 1975, and here I am thirty-three years later and I do not get headaches. I was instantly healed and have been free ever since that day. To me this is a miracle. I hear people, even children, say, "I have a headache" or "I am getting a headache" and I tell them that I don't get headaches and I have been freed for a long time.

There are times when I begin to feel some symptoms of a headache, and at that moment I remind myself of the work the Lord has done in me. And the symptoms go away immediately. Nothing lingers. There is no labor or positive confession. It is just a complete healing that can be traced back to the day I heard a testimony of God's mercy and compassion over another person. Testimonies are a powerful source of encouragement and praise to God.

How did I position myself?

1. I was at the meeting, not at home or anywhere else.
2. I heard and believed that what God had done for her, He could do for me.
3. No one laid their hands on me or prayed for me. I simply believed.
4. I continued to confess my healing and not allow these symptoms to get out of control.

This is not faith in my faith or faith in her faith. It is faith in the Lord and His word through a testimony.

Bridge of Hope Miracle

In India there is a children's outreach program called Bridge of Hope. It is part of the Gospel for Asia mission network. This is a testimony of a little boy named Nibun who came home with a story about Jesus the miracle worker.

Pastor Samuel Jagat runs one of the Bridge of Hope centers in his village. He had no idea that the group of thirty-five Dalit[8] and low-caste children attending would make such a remarkable difference in his ministry. But one little first-grade boy in his center was about to show him otherwise.

Nibun's mother had been ill with malaria for a long time. Doctors, priests and sorcerers could not find a cure, and her death seemed inevitable. But Nibun had a little seed of hope in his heart—God's word. Bible stories were a regular part of the Bridge of Hope curriculum at the center and like many other children, Nibun

---

[8] Dalits (street children), also known as the Untouchables, are the lowest caste of Hinduism. For three thousand years, hundreds of millions of India's Untouchables have suffered oppression, slavery, and countless atrocities. They are trapped in a caste system that denies them adequate education, safe drinking water, decent-paying jobs, and the right to own land or a home. Segregated and oppressed, Dalits are frequently the victims of violent crimes. Revolution in world Missions K.P. Yohanna © 2004 Published by GFA books, a division of Gospel for Asia. Carrollton, TX.

would come home and narrate every story he had heard to his family.

One night, as Nibun and his family sat together beside his mother's bed, he told them how Jesus raised a widow's son from the dead. It became a turning point in all their lives.

"That night, after hearing this story," Nibun's father later shared, "I could not sleep. This story was burning in my heart again and again."

Nibun's father sought out Pastor Samuel the next morning. After hearing more about Jesus and His offer of salvation, the man asked the pastor to come and pray for his wife. "I believe Jesus will heal my wife just as He did the widow's son," he affirmed.

Nibun's mother, though weak in body, shared the same confidence: "My son has talked about Jesus many times in our home. I believe Jesus will heal me."

Pastor Samuel laid hands on the dying woman and prayed for the Lord to raise her up. Then he returned to his home. The next day he saw Nibun and asked how his mother was doing. "My mommy is walking around," he reported happily, "and this morning she prepared breakfast for us!"

When Samuel arrived at Nibun's house, he found a family transformed both physically and spiritually. They had all made a decision to follow Christ.

Nibun's father expressed it this way; "I thank God for this center and pray that He will use it to bring His light into many homes, just as He has done in our family."

In this story you see that Nibun's father took a step of faith. Acting on the story he had heard about Jesus, he called for Pastor Samuel. He confessed that he believed Jesus would heal his wife, and the mother confessed as well, in her own words, "I believe Jesus will heal me." And Jesus did.

They heard and believed and positioned themselves for this miracle by calling the pastor and receiving prayer. They could have brushed away this school child's story, but they did not.

Reprinted and used with permission from Gospel for Asia and Y. P. Yohannan.

11

Restoring Sight to the Blind

> As Jesus went on from there, two blind men followed Him, crying out, "Have mercy on us, Son of David!" When He entered the house, the blind men came up to Him, and Jesus said to them, "Do you believe that I am able to do this?" They said to Him, "Yes, Lord." Then He touched their eyes, saying, "It shall be done to you according to your faith." And their eyes were opened. And Jesus sternly warned them: "See that no one knows *about this*!" But they went out and spread the news about Him throughout all that land. (Matthew 9:27–31)

Not only did people come to Jesus with all kinds of needs but from all kinds of backgrounds and in all kinds of numbers. How did these blind men know that Jesus was able to restore their sight? I think they heard the testimonies of others and the miracles Jesus had done for other people. Old and young alike, Jew and Gentile, and based on those testimonies these blind men were determined to follow Jesus and request a healing.

It is hard to follow if you cannot see. I am sure that there had to be a crowd around Jesus, but in spite of these things or hindrances, they pressed on to get as close to Jesus as possible—close enough to call on Him.

How did they position themselves?

- They heard of Jesus and believed that they could receive a miracle from the Lord. They came based on what they had heard.
- They acted on their belief by following Jesus. Even when He went indoors, they did not give up. They followed Him and pressed in. They were willing to go all the way. I don't know if they were invited in or not, but there they went right in and right up to Jesus.
- They opened their mouths and called on Jesus. The Bible says, "To You they cried out and were delivered; In You they trusted and were not disappointed" (Psalm 22:5).
- They were asking for mercy, which is unmerited favor. There was no demand on their part.
- When Jesus asked them if they believed that He could do this, they did not hesitate. They said, "Yes, Lord."

Jesus touched them, and their sight was restored.

Here you have two men who could not see, and yet they managed to position themselves for a miracle. Others have their sight and yet can't or do not even try to position or press in to get a miracle. If these blind men could position themselves, then we can too.

They were blind, but they had faith. Jesus asks them, *"Do you believe that I am able to do this?"* and they did not hesitate. They said, "Yes, Lord." Then He touched their eyes and said, "According to your faith will it be done to you"

In his book on winning souls, Spurgeon said, "According to your faith be it unto you," is one of the unalterable laws of His kingdom.

"According to your faith, will it be done to you." Do you have faith? Even if your faith is as small as mustard, seed it will be enough to move a mountain. It is not always the size of your faith that matters, but that you have faith.

12

Jesus Heals the Epileptic Boy

When they came back to the disciples, they saw
a large crowd around them, and some scribes
arguing with them. Immediately, when the
entire crowd saw Him, they were amazed and
began running up to greet Him. And He asked
them, "What are you discussing with them?"
And one of the crowd answered Him, "Teacher,
I brought You my son, possessed with a spirit
which makes him mute; and whenever it seizes
him, it slams him to the ground and he foams
at the mouth, and grinds his teeth and stiffens
out. I told Your disciples to cast it out, and they
could not do it." And He answered them and said,
"O unbelieving generation, how long shall I be
with you? How long shall I put up with you? Bring
him to Me!" They brought the boy to Him. When
he saw Him, immediately the spirit threw him
into a convulsion, and falling to the ground, he
began rolling around and foaming at the mouth.
And He asked his father, "How long has this
been happening to him?" And he said, "From
childhood. "It has often thrown him both into

the fire and into the water to destroy him. But if You can do anything, take pity on us and help us!" And Jesus said to him, " 'If You can?' All things are possible to him who believes." Immediately the boy's father cried out and said, "I do believe; help my unbelief." When Jesus saw that a crowd was rapidly gathering, He rebuked the unclean spirit, saying to it, "You deaf and mute spirit, I command you, come out of him and do not enter him again." After crying out and throwing him into terrible convulsions, it came out; and the boy became so much like a corpse that most of them said, "He is dead!" But Jesus took him by the hand and raised him; and he got up. (Mark 9:14–27)

I am glad that Jesus can see beyond our weaknesses and see our need!

This man was looking for help. He came to Jesus, "Teacher I brought you my son" (v.17). He told the disciples in verse 18 to cast out the spirit, but they could not. When others can't help, we should not stop until we reach Jesus.

The man asked for pity in verse 22. He asked for pity and asked Jesus for help. In verse 23, Jesus said to him, "If you can? All things are possible to him who believes." The man had some reservations, and we can relate. There are those times when we are hoping and trying to believe, yet there is that feeling or nagging doubt that keeps us at a distance. But even with his unbelief, this man asked for help.

He positioned himself by asking for help with his unbelief. You see the disciples had already tried and did not come through, so I think this affected the man's level of faith. He may have thought if others could not, maybe Jesus would not be able to help.

Jesus took this boy by the hand and raised him (v. 27). Praise God! I see that this again was treated as a spirit more than an illness. Regardless, Jesus has authority over unclean spirits. All three gospel writers, Matthew, Mark, and Luke, reported this incident with the unclean demonic spirit giving testimony to the fact that some illnesses are brought on by spiritual forces.

Praise God that, "Jesus summoned His twelve disciples and gave them authority over unclean spirits, to cast them out, and to heal every kind of disease and every kind of sickness" (Matthew 10:1). This verse shows us that Jesus has authority over unclean spirits and has the authority to heal every kind of disease and sickness. Here again we see that the scriptures teach us that some people are sick with diseases and others are afflicted with unclean spirits.

This is the testimony of Jesus, "You know of Jesus of Nazareth, how God anointed Him with the Holy Spirit and with power, and how He went about doing good and healing all who were oppressed by the devil, for God was with Him" (Acts 10:38).

Notice that this verse says that, "Jesus went about healing all who were oppressed by the devil." These are an interesting choice of words, "healing all who were oppressed by the devil." Jesus had no problem with the fact that even the man recognized his son's condition as something of a spiritual nature and that it needed to be cast out.

This man somehow knew that he was dealing with a spirit. I don't know how he knew this, but he did. That fact did not stop him from seeking help, and maybe that's why he sought help from Jesus. Remember the words of Jesus when it came to this man?

He said, "All things are possible to him who believes" (v. 23). "He (Jesus) rebuked the unclean spirit, saying to it, 'You deaf and mute spirit, I command you, come out of him and do not enter him again'" (v. 25). Some people call this a deliverance, while others call it a healing. As for me, I'm just glad that Jesus answered and the boy was made well.

I know that there is Satanic and demonic spiritual activity when it comes to some illnesses. I have seen my share of these things and have also seen the power of God release, heal, and restore those who have suffered under such conditions. We need to remember what Jesus said to this man: "All things are possible to him who believes."

As you can see, the scriptures are full of miracles in both the Old and New Testaments. Why is such a large portion of the Bible dedicated to these stories regarding miracles? I believe it is to reveal to us God's will when it comes to miracles and healings. These stories and testimonies point to the love and mercy of God toward men. They also point to the redemptive power of God. He redeems and restores.

What did these people have in common with each other? They were in need of heavenly intervention. They had exhausted their resources and had already gone to others for help, even doctors, but did not get the help they needed. They were children, fathers, mothers, friends, royal officials, centurions, young, old, rich, poor, believers, and nonbelievers, people just like you and me in every way. And God had mercy on them.

We need to get back to a place where we are not only believing for miracles, but whenever necessary, we need to position ourselves for it. Our faith should never be in what we do to position ourselves; it should always be in Jesus and His love and mercy.

Miracle in My Family
Dale Hanson Burke

I am not sure that I ever believed in miracles until one happened in my family. It's not that I didn't believe in God or see Him at work in my life. It's just that I had never before personally witnessed a moment when God intervened and upset the course of nature. In my heart I knew that he was capable of doing so, but my mind always got in the way of accepting it.

Then, one day, just as I was coming to grips with the fact that my vibrant, loving father would soon die, God interrupted the course of nature. My father's brain tumor, which the doctors just months before had called "highly malignant, fast-growing, and inoperable," suddenly disappeared.

My father's neurosurgeon, an atheist, didn't hesitate to call it a miracle. But I didn't dare to begin to hope, even though all of the tests that had confirmed the original diagnosis now confirmed the absence of the tumor. It hadn't just stopped growing. It had shrunk to the point that it was barely detectable. I wanted to be happy, but mostly I was shocked.

I had been taught to "pray in faith, believing" (Matthew 21:22), but I recognized that mostly I prayed in fear, hoping. Sometimes I prayed in despair, doubting. During those times, the only prayer that came to me was, "Help thou mine unbelief" (Mark 9:24 KJV). I despaired in my limited ability to look directly at glory without turning away.

My father's miracle gave us unexpected extra months to be with him. But then another tumor appeared, and this one didn't go away. Eventually my father died two and a half years after the original prognosis that had given him fewer than three months to live. Yet despite our grief, my family knew that we had been witnesses to a miracle. We probably understand miracles less now than we did before my father's healing. But we do know that they happen.

There are many examples of miracles in the Bible, and I read them now with new understanding. People seemed to accept blind men suddenly seeing or the dead coming back to life. But as I read those accounts now, I put myself into the situations and always my reaction is the same: I would be one of the doubters, not one of those who so easily believed.

Jesus upset the natural order of things in a profound way. He didn't do the predictable or the understandable. Witnessing a miracle doesn't make it any more understandable. But I have witnessed one, and I know that miracles don't just change the course of events; they change hearts. And perhaps that is the greatest miracle.[9]

---

[9] Dale Hanson Bourke is president of CIDZ Foundation in Washington, DC. The CIDRZ Foundation (pronounced "ciders") began in 2006 to provide support to individuals and organizations fighting diseases in Africa.
This story first appeared in "Turn Toward the Wind," copyright Dale Hanson Bourke. Used by permission of the author.

13

Reach Out and Touch

A woman who had had a hemorrhage for twelve years, and had endured much at the hands of many physicians, and had spent all that she had and was not helped at all, but rather had grown worse—after hearing about Jesus, she came up in the crowd behind Him and touched His cloak. For she thought, "If I just touch His garments, I will get well." Immediately the flow of her blood was dried up; and she felt in her body that she was healed of her affliction. Immediately Jesus, perceiving in Himself that the power proceeding from Him had gone forth, turned around in the crowd and said, "Who touched My garments?" And His disciples said to Him, "You see the crowd pressing in on You, and You say, 'Who touched Me?'" And He looked around to see the woman who had done this. But the woman fearing and trembling, aware of what had happened to her, came and fell down before Him and told Him the whole truth. And He said to her, "Daughter, your faith has made you well; go in peace and be healed of your affliction." (Mark 5:25–34)

Here is a woman who had to go beyond herself to receive a miracle from Jesus. We are not told her name, but we are told of her condition. She was suffering from a hemorrhage for twelve long years. Not only that, but as a result of her search for relief, she "endured much at the hands of many physicians." If that wasn't bad enough, she had spent all she had and found no help or healing.

Obviously she was a woman of means. She was able to go to "many physicians" and "spent all she had." This tells me that she had already tried everything within her power to get healed. But this woman was not one to just give up or settle for things as they were.

She made a decision based on what she had heard about Jesus. In verse 27 it says "after hearing about Jesus." She heard about Jesus but it does not tell as what she heard. If you read Mark 5 there are a number of miracles happening before this woman came to Jesus. Based on the story, I believe that she heard of the healings and miracles He had done for others and thought that she too could receive a miracle.

In fact, the crowd that was around Him was there because of what they had heard. This reminds me of what the apostle Peter said in Acts 10:38: "You know of Jesus of Nazareth, how God anointed Him with the Holy Spirit and with power, and how He went about doing good and healing all who were oppressed by the devil, for God was with Him."

Jesus had a reputation for healing and performing miracles. So she set herself up to receive a miracle:

- She acted on what she had heard about Jesus.
- She pushed her way through the crowd (overcame her obstacles).

- She thought to herself that she would get healed (confession).
- Sometimes you have to talk to yourself and take control of the negative thoughts.
- She reached out and touched Jesus (faith reaches out).

This woman saw the crowd and did not let that discourage her. She pushed her way to Jesus and reached out as far as she could with all her might and was able to touch the fringe of His garment, and got healed. "Immediately the flow of her blood was dried up; and she felt in her body that she was healed of her affliction" (v. 29). This is what I call positioning yourself.

Notice that Jesus does not rebuke her for her actions. Instead He acknowledges her and confirms her healing. "And He said to her, 'Daughter, your faith has made you well; go in peace and be healed of your affliction'" (v. 34).

Sometimes we need to just reach out by faith.

14

The Miracle of Children

My wife's sister came to live with us one summer after she had been in the army. During her stay she shared with us that she could not have children. After having tried several times, she was told that she would not be able to conceive.

We shared some testimonies with her about God's amazing love and power to heal and to give the barren children. After sharing with her that I believed in God's ability to perform miracles, I offered to pray for her that she would have a child. I laid hands on her and began to pray for the miracle of children. I asked God for mercy and prayed for blessings in the name of Jesus.

Within a year she had her first child, a boy. She was overjoyed. Then she conceived again and had another boy. Again she was just beside herself. Then she had her third child, another boy. After the third child, she came back and asked us to stop praying for her or to ask God to hold off on the miracles. We laughed, as we thought to ourselves, *Well, you asked for it!*

After having her fourth child—you guessed it, another boy—she stopped having children. This was the first time I had prayed for someone to have children.

I shared that testimony with the church while I was preaching, and a woman came forward asking for prayer because she was barren. The doctors told her that she would never have children. I prayed for her, and that year she conceived and bore her first child, a boy. She only had one child, but that was enough. She had received her miracle.

The third woman was new to our ministry and wanted to have children so bad that she had gone to many doctors, including some doctors in Mexico, where there are some treatments that are not practiced here in the United States.

After several disappointments and much suffering, she decided to seek the Lord for help. She came and confessed her desire and how far she had gone to get help, but found none. She showed us the doctors' reports that she had with her from the United States and from Mexico. After hearing the word of God and growing in the faith, she said that now she knew that the only one who could possibly help her was Jesus. She asked for prayer. That day I asked some of the woman in the church to come and lay hands on her and pray.

These women surrounded her as sisters in Christ and began to pray. Several months later we all stood to praise God as we heard her testify that she was pregnant. The glow on her face was amazing. She went through a tough labor, but at the end she gave birth to a lovely healthy baby boy.

These women positioned themselves for their miracles. They confessed their needs and desires before the Lord. They asked for prayer and waited on the Lord. It took some humility to confess barrenness and the inability to conceive, but they did. They surrendered to the Lord, and He delivered.

Six boys in all.

15

The Ten Lepers A Second Chance to Live

While He was on the way to Jerusalem, He was passing between Samaria and Galilee. As He entered a village, ten leprous men who stood at a distance met Him; and they raised their voices, saying, "Jesus, Master, have mercy on us!" When He saw them, He said to them, "Go and show yourselves to the priests." And as they were going, they were cleansed. Now one of them, when he saw that he had been healed, turned back, glorifying God with a loud voice, and he fell on his face at His feet, giving thanks to Him. And he was a Samaritan. Then Jesus answered and said, "Were there not ten cleansed? But the nine—where are they? "Was no one found who returned to give glory to God, except this foreigner?" And He said to him, "Stand up and go; your faith has made you well." (Luke 17:11–20)

As you can see, there are times when it is just one person looking for a Miracle, and there are times when it is more than one at a time. Jesus saw the fact that there were ten, and when He gave the word, all ten of them were instantly cleansed.

How did these men position themselves for this miracle?

1. They heard the reports of what Jesus was able to do and stepped out in faith to find Him.
2. Even though they were at a distance, they did not let this stop them. They raised their voices loud enough to be heard.
3. They asked for mercy (unmerited favor). They made no claim on Him. They just asked for mercy.

They took the time and made the journey. They got within earshot of the master and opened their mouths to ask for what they did not deserve. They asked for a miracle. And it is amazing to see that all ten of them were cleansed at the same time.

We don't know who these men were. There does not seem to be anything special about them that required an audience with Jesus. They were just people with a deep need, and Jesus answered with a word and healed them.

The one that makes this story unique is this Samaritan. He had enough in him to acknowledge the fact that he received what he did not deserve and came back to humble himself and give praise to God.

You would think that these ten lepers would be filled with thankfulness and overjoyed at the fact that their death sentence had been removed. Lepers had a short life expectancy, and Jesus, with just a word, changed that. He gave them a second chance at life.

I don't know and can't understand how these lepers could just walk away and not feel compelled to reach back, come back, and humble themselves before the Lord with tears of joy and expressions of gratitude that their lives had been extended. They could return home to be reunited with their families and friends. They could now return to their jobs and dream again. They could now be part of the community they once knew.

Maybe this is all they had in mind, and they just lost themselves in the moment as they saw the many possibilities before them. Perhaps they did not want to waste time with something as small and insignificant as giving thanks to the Lord for what He had done.

There are so many people who, after having received such a great healing or miracle, just fail to acknowledge God or give Him any praise. Notice that this one leper stands out above the rest in this story Jesus asked him, "Where are the others?" And then he went on to recognize his faith and make him well.

Take time to glory and give praise to God for what He has done in your life. Don't be like the nine who just walked away.

16

The Second Touch

> And they came to Bethsaida And they brought a blind man to Jesus and implored Him to touch him. Taking the blind man by the hand, He brought him out of the village; and after spitting on his eyes and laying His hands on him, He asked him, "Do you see anything?" And he looked up and said, "I see men, for I see them like trees, walking around." Then again He laid His hands on his eyes; and he looked intently and was restored, and began to see everything clearly." (Mark 8:22–25)

Sometimes we need more than one touch from God for the miracle or healing to come to a complete state.

After feeding four thousand people, arguing with the Pharisees, and warning His disciples about the false doctrines of the Pharisees and Herod, Jesus's attention was drawn to the need of a blind man. It is amazing how Jesus can focus on one man and give him personal attention—showing him compassion and love. As you can see, Jesus had the ability to care for four thousand or just one.

There are those who are physically blind, and there are those who are spiritually and emotionally blind. Examples of spiritual and emotional blindness include those who have anger, bitterness, jealousy, fear, doubt, depression, loneliness, and unforgiveness. All these things and others like them can lead to blindness and Jesus is the only one who can heal you and help you to see again with clarity.

> And they came to Bethsaida and they brought a blind man to Jesus and implored Him to touch him. Taking the blind man by the hand, He brought him out of the village; and after spitting on his eyes and laying His hands on him, He asked him, "Do you see anything?" And he looked up and said, "I see men, for I see them like trees, walking around." Then again He laid His hands on his eyes; and he looked intently and was restored, and began to see everything clearly.

Some people brought a blind man to Jesus. We don't know who brought the man. Bringing someone who could not see to Jesus was an act of love by his friends. You see, there are those who know you are blind and leave you there, or maybe they don't know where to take you to get help. This man had real friends. He met Jesus, the greatest friend in all of history. And what does Jesus do?

1. He does not push him away. Remember, Jesus was busy and perhaps tired. He had just fed four thousand people. He had just experienced discord with the Pharisees. He had been teaching the disciples, and yet He made time for this one man and his need.
2. He took him by the hand and led him away from the crowd and gave him His undivided attention.

3. Jesus spat in his eyes. This was necessary as back in those days, not having the wonderful technology we have today, the eyelids needed to be separated. This did not need a miracle: it just needed a little spit. Notice that Jesus took care of the natural first.

4. Finally, He performed the miracle by restoring the man's sight. After Jesus laid His hands on the man, He asked him, "Do you see anything?"

   The man replied, "I see men, for I see them like trees, walking around." From this statement we can conclude that the man may have had the ability to see at one time because he could distinguish between trees and men. Someone who has never had sight needs to be helped at first to distinguish between things as even their own reflection can shock them.

   And now comes the best part of this event. Jesus did not give up on him. He had not yet received the full impact of the healing and needed a second touch. I am glad that Jesus did not leave the man in this hazy condition but brought him to a complete healing.

5. Jesus laid His hands on the man again. Thank God for the second touch! Thank God for the second chance for another opportunity to get right with God and recover our spiritual sight. Jesus wants to restore you and help you see again.

Some of you have lost your sight because of sin, anger, bitterness, pain, abuse, rape, and other things, like drugs and sex. I want you to know that God still loves you and is ready to touch your life again.

Will you let Jesus touch you again and help you to see?

Brother Jesse's Miracle

A young lady in our church asked me if I could talk to her brother and help him. She went on to tell me that he was a heroin addict and in trouble with the law. I agreed to go and meet him. My goal was to share the gospel with him, hoping that he would come to Christ and be delivered from his addictions.

I went to their home and met the young man. His name was Jesus Caldero (nickname) Jesse. We talked for a while, and I began to tell him about God's love and how God had a plan for his life. I went on to tell him about God's power and how the Lord had set me free from drugs and alcohol.

I talked about how He set the captives free, and then I said that God could even set people free from the hands of a judge. I don't know why I said that, but there it was. He looked at me and asked if I really believed that God could set him free from the hands of a judge. I said yes.

At that moment he said, "Well, I have to appear before a judge tomorrow, and I want you to come with me. To tell the truth, at that moment I felt trapped. I did not know that this was his situation. I swallowed hard and said that I would go with him to the courthouse.

I pressed on to see if he would accept Jesus as his Savior, but he would not. Well needless to say, I went home and prayed and asked God for a miracle because I did not know what I was in for. This young man did not receive my witness, and I had no experience when it came to helping someone with the court system. I did not even know what he was accused of, but I prayed and got up early to go with him in the name of the Lord.

When I arrived at the courthouse, he was consulting his lawyer. Before I greeted him and his sister, I heard the lawyer say that the charges were many and that this was a hanging judge and he would have to look forward to serving some time because he was now an adult.

Then the lawyer asked them who I was, and they said I was a pastor of a church and a friend of the family. The lawyer looked at me and said, "When they call his case, you get up and stand with him." I agreed.

I did not know what to expect. I heard some of the charges and thought to myself, *This guy is in deep trouble.* My hands began to sweat, and I began to pray.

I knew that Jesse was hanging on the words, "God can set people free from the hands of a judge." I knew that that's why he wanted me there. But I did not know what God would do.

After several other cases had been called where I heard the judge handing out sentences, Jesse's name was called. I stood up and went forward with the lawyer. The judge started to read some of the charges and told him that he could give him six to ten years. Then he looked over his shoulder and asked me, "Who are you?"

I started to say my name and that I was a pastor, and he shouted at me to speak louder. I started again. This time I raised my voice and said, "I am the pastor of Pure in Heart Church, my name is Peter Negron, and I am here because I believe that we can help this young man. He may be guilty of these charges and you could send him to jail, but I believe that he is a drug addict and sending him to jail will not help with his problem."

He asked me what I had to offer, and by faith I said that I would help him with a program in Chicago called Teen Challenge that works directly with drug addicts. I knew of the program but had no formal relationship with them and had not talked to them about this young man. I was speaking by faith.

The judge looked at him and then looked at me. Then he said to him, "I could send you away right now for a long time, but I am going to release you to this man and this program." Then the judge looked at me again and said. "If he does not listen to you and he does not work with this program, you call me and I will have him arrested and sent straight to prison."

He addressed Jesse and said, "You better do whatever this man says. He has the authority to call me, and I will put you away. Now get out of my courtroom."

We walked away with his lawyer following us and saying over and over again, "It's a miracle! It's a miracle! This judge does not let people go, especially with a case like yours."

God can set people free from the hands of a judge, even when they are guilty. This is the mercy and grace of God. Well we rejoiced, but our celebration hit a bump in the road. We went straight to Teen Challenge, and after the interview with this young man, we were told that they would not have a bed until Monday and this was Friday. Can you imagine what a drug addict can do in one weekend?

I can. You see this is the world I grew up in. I was worried and asked his family to keep him home and watch him carefully to make sure that he did not leave the home and get in trouble with the law again.

Well at 11:00 p.m., I got a call. He had escaped, and no one knew his whereabouts. This led me back to praying and asking God for help. Saturday went by and then Sunday was a long day with no news on where he could possibly be. Then early Monday morning, his sister called me to tell me that he came home and was ready to go with me to Teen Challenge. I picked him up, and we went and got him enrolled in the program.

The administrator told us that he could not have any contact with anyone for two weeks. After that time, his family and I would be allowed to see him. Two weeks went by, and I was finally able to go and visit with him. I got there and was asked to wait while he was notified of my visit.

A few moments later I saw a young man with a smile on his face as I heard him call me "Brother Peter." You see, during those two weeks, he had come to know Jesus as his personal Savior and, now I was not just a pastor in the community, or a friend to the family. I was now his brother in Christ.

This is one of the greatest miracles I have witnessed. I saw this young man with a new face, a new heart, a new joy, and a new life. He was transformed from the inside out, and he was radiant. He was full of life. In just a few short weeks, what had been a life of addiction and crime came to an end. Second Corinthians 5:17

says, "Therefore if anyone is in Christ, he is a new creature; the old things passed away; behold, new things have come."

Jesse had his sins forgiven. He became a new creation. He was free from drugs, free from the courts, and free to live life again. As I always say, God is good!

The greatest miracle of all is that of a transformed life through the power of God. What we call the miracle of being born again. "Blessed be the God and Father of our Lord Jesus Christ, who according to His great mercy has caused us to be born again to a living hope through the resurrection of Jesus Christ from the dead" (1 Peter 1:3).

After this several members of Jesse's family came to know the Lord Jesus Christ as Savior and Lord and continue to walk in the faith today.

Miracles: Were They Only to Confirm the Apostles?
By Mike Peters

When I entered seminary, I learned that noncharismatics use the word *miracles* differently than do charismatics. Noncharismatics use the word *miracles* to refer to the works of the apostles that validated them as divine messengers. Miracles, to noncharismatics, are always designed to authenticate the human instrument through whom God has chosen to declare a specific revelation.

Charismatics, on the other hand, define miracles as any supernatural act of God. To charismatics, miracles were not solely for the purpose of confirming the apostles as divine messengers. Miracles might be for the purpose of glorifying God, blessing a person, or furthering the work of the gospel.

This difference of definition produces some confusion. When charismatics refer to a miracle, noncharismatics often think they are referring to something that validates someone as a divine messenger. Charismatics do not refer to miracles this way, nor do they believe that those God uses to perform miracles are divine messengers on par with the apostles.

Definition

Some of the differences between charismatics and noncharismatics are reduced to definitions. How you define miracles determines whether you believe they continue today. If you define miracles as supernatural acts that confirm divine messengers, then you believe that miracles ceased upon the completion of the New Testament. On the other hand, if you define miracles as any supernatural act, then you believe that miracles continue today.

If you define a miracle as authenticating a divine messenger, then no matter how supernatural something is, if it does not authenticate someone, it cannot be a miracle. This would exclude creation and the flood from being miracles:

> Creation, the Flood, natural wonders, and cataclysms show God clearly at work supernaturally interceding in human affairs, judging rebellious people, and blessing those who are faithful. Such things are not miracles by the definition we have given.[10]

Many Christians, not just charismatics, would not concur with a definition that rejects creation and the flood as miracles. The theologian Millard Erickson stated that miracles are "those special supernatural works of God's providence, which are not explicable on the basis of the usual patterns of nature." [11] According to Erickson, miracles are supernatural works of God that are unexplainable according to the laws of nature.

---

[10] John MacArthur, *Charismatic Chaos*, 106–07.

[11] Millard J. Erickson, *Christian Theology* (Grand Rapids, MI: Baker Book House. 1990), 406.

This definition is larger and includes all of God's works beyond the patterns of nature. For example, it was not natural for the Red Sea to part. It was not natural for flocks of quail to fall upon Israel. It was not natural for the axe head to float to the surface when Elisha prayed. It was not natural for the loaves and the fish to multiply in Jesus's hands. In fact, the Bible itself is not natural. It is not natural for men to write a divinely inspired book. If miracles are God's supernatural works that do not follow the usual patterns of nature, then the Bible tells us all kinds of miracles, and the Bible itself is a miracle.

This means that miracles surpass the laws of nature or the results of nature's laws. When the axe head rose to the surface of the water, God did not suspend the law of gravity. Everything else stayed in place (2 Kings 6:4--7). God simply lifted the axe head and in so doing superseded the law of gravity. On another occasion, God affected a miracle by supernaturally using the laws of nature to surpass their normal results. A strong wind drove quail to the nation of Israel (Psalm 78:26–29). Wind is natural, but God supernaturally used it beyond its normal pattern to drive quail to Israel. This too is referred to as a miracle by the theologian Lewis Berkhof: "If God in the performance of a miracle did sometimes utilize forces that were present in nature, He used them in a way that was out of the ordinary, to produce unexpected results, and it was exactly this that constituted the miracle."[12]

Christians who define miracles as God's supernatural acts that are not explainable on the basis of the usual patterns of nature believe that miracles continue today. Whereas, Christians who define miracles as authenticating signs restrict miracles to the apostolic age.

---

[12] Lewis Berkhof, *Systematic Theology* (Grand Rapids, MI: Eerdmans Publishing Co., 1977) 176–77.

Those who restrict miracles to the apostolic age still believe that God works supernaturally today. They simply define it as something other than a miracle. The Puritans referred to such works of God as extraordinary providence. Ordinary providence occurred when God worked according to the laws of nature. Extraordinary providence occurred when God worked in a manner that superseded the laws of nature. To a charismatic, extraordinary providence sounds just like a miracle.

Purpose of Miracles

The question regarding miracles is not so much about whether God performs them but for what purpose He performs them. Or if you believe they ceased, you might ask for what purpose did He perform them? The writer of Hebrews tells us that God gave signs and wonders for a definite purpose:

> How shall we escape if we neglect so great a salvation, which at first began to be spoken by the Lord, and was confirmed to us by those who heard Him. God also bearing witness both with signs and wonders, with various gifts of the Holy Spirit, according to His will. (Hebrews 2:3–4)

The words *was confirming* are in the past tense, and to those who believe miracles ceased with the Apostles, this means to them that miracles were for the purpose of confirming the apostles as divine messengers: "Here is a clear biblical word that the miracles, wonders, and sign gifts were given only to the first-generation apostles to confirm that they were messengers of a new revelation."[13]

---

[13] John MacArtur, *Charismatic Chaos*, 119.

It is true that the word *confirmed* is in the past tense, but it is not referring to miracles as having confirmed the apostles as divine messengers. It is referring to the apostles as having confirmed the gospel as the divine message. The writer of Hebrews was not one of the original apostles. While many believe that it was Paul, others say that it was someone else. All concur that the writer was not one of the Twelve. This is important because the writer of Hebrews referred to the Twelve when he stated that the gospel "was confirmed to us by those [Twelve] who heard Him [Jesus]" (Hebrews 2:3).

The Twelve heard Christ while He walked on earth. This was approximately thirty-five years before the writing of Hebrews. Hebrews was written just prior to the destruction of Jerusalem in AD 70. During the thirty-five years between Christ's crucifixion and the writing of Hebrews, the Twelve confirmed the message that Christ spoke. This explains why the statement "it was confirmed" is in the past tense.

The past tense does not imply that miracles ceased. It refers back to the thirty-five-year period between Christ first speaking the message and the apostles confirming it. The Twelve had already confirmed the message of salvation by preaching the gospel prior to the writing of Hebrews. Therefore, these passages do not teach that miracles confirmed the apostles, but that the apostles confirmed the message spoken by the Lord.

The twelve were not the only ones to confirm the Lord's words. God also confirmed the words spoken by the Lord with "signs, wonders, and various miracles and gifts of the Holy Spirit" (Hebrews 2:4). Significantly, God's confirming miracles are not past tense but present tense. He is "bearing witness." "Bearing witness" is a present and actively bearing witness. The apostles "bore witness." God is "bearing witness."

The Lord was the first to speak of this great salvation. The apostles who heard Jesus confirmed what the Lord spoke, and God is bearing witness to this great salvation "with both signs, wonders and various miracles and gifts of the Holy Spirit." Miracles confirm this great salvation.

Today, miracles serve the same purpose they did in the apostles' day. They bear witness to the salvation of the Lord. God still performs miracles because today is the day of salvation. Salvation starts with a miracle. A person needs a miracle to be born again. Christians need daily miracles of grace to walk in obedience to Jesus Christ. Miracles are needed to overcome sickness. When facing death, it requires faith in a miraculous God that receives the soul into glory. Everything from new birth to glorification requires a miracle. Martin Luther described conversion as the greatest miracle:

> Conversion is the greatest of all miracles. Everyday witnesses miracles after miracle; that any village adheres to the Gospel when a hundred thousand devils are arrayed against it, or that the truth is maintained in this wicked world, is a continued miracle to which healing the sick or raising the dead is a mere trifle. [14]

Somewhere today, the miracle of conversion will supernaturally raise from death to life a spiritually dead person. If God supernaturally raises an eternally dead soul, why is it difficult to accept that He miraculously heals bodies? If we can believe the greater, why is it difficult to believe the lesser? Charismatics and noncharismatics believe God for miracles every day as they lead people to the Lord Jesus Christ.

---

[14] Cited in Charles Hodges, *Systematic Theology* (Grand Rapids, MI: Eerdmans Publishing Co., 1981) vol. 1, 617.

Although the scripture is complete and there is no longer a need for divine messengers like the Twelve, there is continuing need for miracles. Noncharismatics may choose to call such miracles "extraordinary providence" while charismatics refer to such works as miracles. Nevertheless, the age of miracles has not ended. You may be one of His miracles.

> This chapter is used with permission from the author Dr. Michael D. Peters, PhD. Taken from the book *The Case for Charismatics,* copyright 2000.

While the scriptures talk about miracles and healings, I don't think we have a right to promise people that if they do all the right things they will get a healing or a miracle. Remember that miracles are up to God.

But because the scriptures do talk about miracles and do not qualify who can and cannot receive a miracle, we can encourage each other to trust God and position ourselves and others for the possibility of miracles.

The one thing that most of these stories have in common is prayer. People prayed. One of the best ways to position yourself for a miracle is to pray. You must humble yourself before God, acknowledging the fact that He is God and that He is able, willing, and ready to help those who call upon Him. When we pray, we are simply saying to God that we are ready to put our trust in Him and no one or nothing else. Some of us call this a step of faith. Call it what you will. Just take that step. You have nothing to lose and everything to gain.

Once again, I want to say that God is the same yesterday, today, and forever, and "It is no secret what God can do, what He's done for others He can do for you."[15]

If you need help praying for a miracle, write me and I will pray with you and for you. The Bible says that the prayer of a righteous man avails much. Sometimes we need others to stand with us in the time of need.

I would like to put together a group of testimonials of those who have been provoked to trust God and His word again and have received a miracle as a direct result of reading this work. Thank you and God bless.

In the words of Warren W. Wiersbe, "Miracles of themselves do not save lost sinners (Luke 16:27–31; John 2:23–25). Miracles must be tied to the message of the word of God."

Be Daring
Acts 13–28
Put your faith where the action is
Published by David C. Cook

Open your heart to Christ today and call on Him to save you. That my friend is the greatest miracle of all.

---

[15] Words from the song by Mahalia Jackson "It Is No Secret What God Can Do."

Printed in the United States
By Bookmasters